Alexander Mackenzie, Explorer
The Hero Who Failed

James K. Smith

"The lords of the lakes and forest have passed away" but their work will endure in the boundaries of the Dominion of Canada. . . .

H. A. Innis, *The Fur Trade in Canada*

McGraw-Hill Ryerson Limited

Toronto Montreal New York London Sydney
Johannesburg Mexico Panama Düsseldorf Singapore
São Paulo Kuala Lumpur New Delhi

By the same author
DAVID THOMPSON: Fur Trader, Explorer, Geographer

Alexander Mackenzie, Explorer

ISBN 0-07-077619-9

Library of Congress Catalog Card Number 73-2359

1 2 3 4 5 6 7 8 9 10 HR 2 1 0 9 8 7 6 5 4 3

Printed and bound in Canada

To the memory of my father

ACKNOWLEDGMENTS

There is an enormous body of literature on the fur trade, and I have benefited from the research and writings of many persons. But I am singularly indebted to the publications of Professor Harold A. Innis and Dr. W. Stewart Wallace of the University of Toronto, Dr. W. Kaye Lamb, former Dominion Archivist, Professor E. E. Rich of St. Catharine's College, Cambridge University, and Mr. Bernard De Voto of the United States. This book owes much to their investigations of the trade and its practitioners.

I also want to express my gratitude to three other people. Mrs. Shirley Marshall and Mrs. Carol Waldock not only typed manuscript drafts, but they retyped various sections of manuscript more times than any one of us probably cares to remember. And Miss Heather Marshall provided me with some shrewd criticism, particularly in the first-draft stage.

J. K. S.

CONTENTS

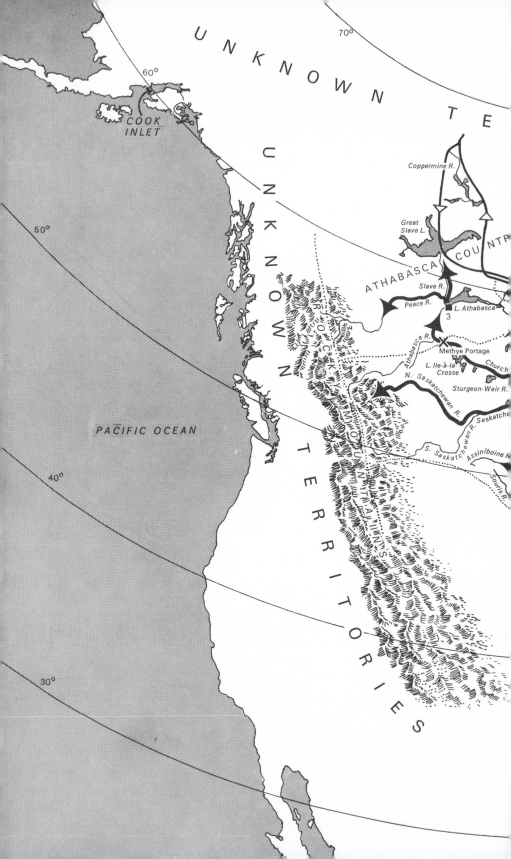

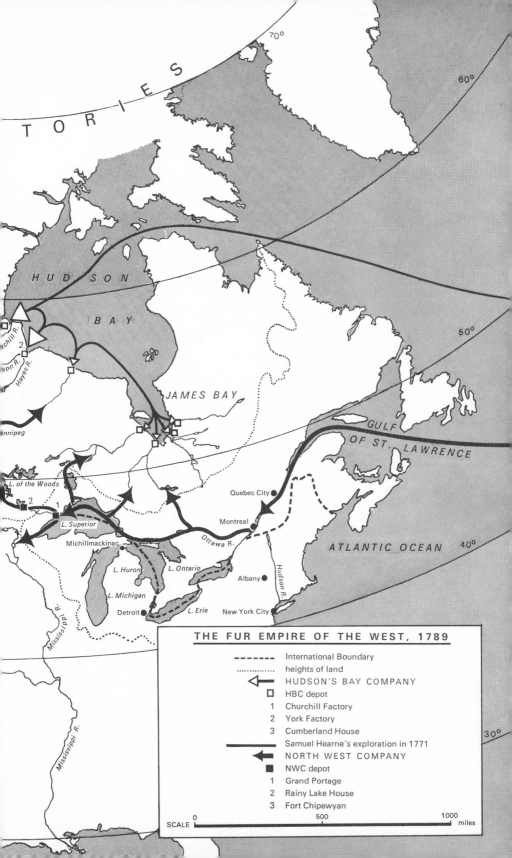

THE FUR EMPIRE OF THE WEST, 1789

- - - - - - - International Boundary
.... heights of land
◁─── HUDSON'S BAY COMPANY
□ HBC depot
1 Churchill Factory
2 York Factory
3 Cumberland House
─── Samuel Hearne's exploration in 1771
◀─── NORTH WEST COMPANY
■ NWC depot
1 Grand Portage
2 Rainy Lake House
3 Fort Chipewyan

SCALE |⎯⎯⎯⎯⎯⎯|⎯⎯⎯⎯⎯⎯| miles
0   500   1000

TORIES

HUDSON

BAY

JAMES BAY

GULF OF ST. LAWRENCE

ATLANTIC OCEAN

Churchill R.
son R.
Hayes R.
nnipeg
L. of the Woods
2   1
L. Superior
Michilimackinac
L. Huron
L. Michigan
L. Ontario
L. Erie
Detroit
Quebec City
Montreal
Ottawa R.
Albany
Hudson R.
New York City
Mississippi R.
Mississippi R.

70°
60°
50°
40°
30°

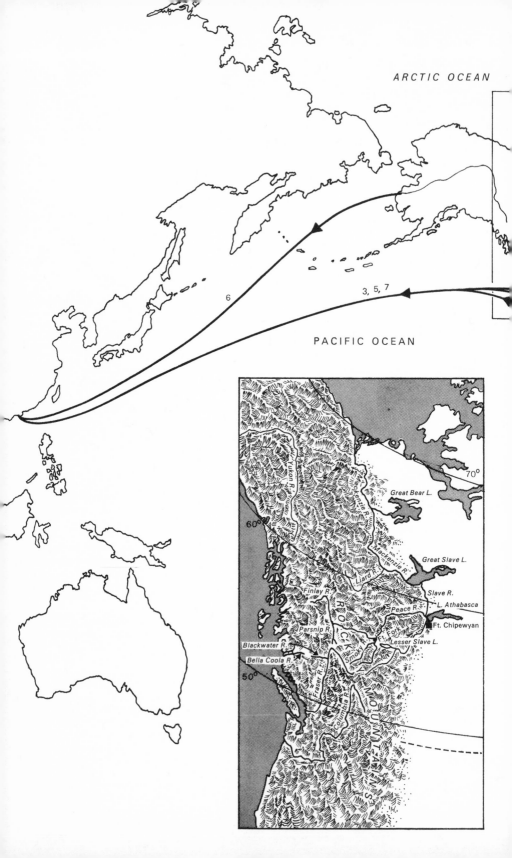

ARCTIC OCEAN

PACIFIC OCEAN

6

3, 5, 7

Yukon R.
Great Bear L.
70°
60°
Mackenzie R.
Great Slave L.
Liard R.
Slave R.
Finlay R.
L. Athabasca
Peace R.
Ft. Chipewyan
Parsnip R.
ROCKY
Fort
Blackwater R.
Lesser Slave L.
Bella Coola R.
Smoky
50°
Fraser R.
Columbia R.
MOUNTAINS

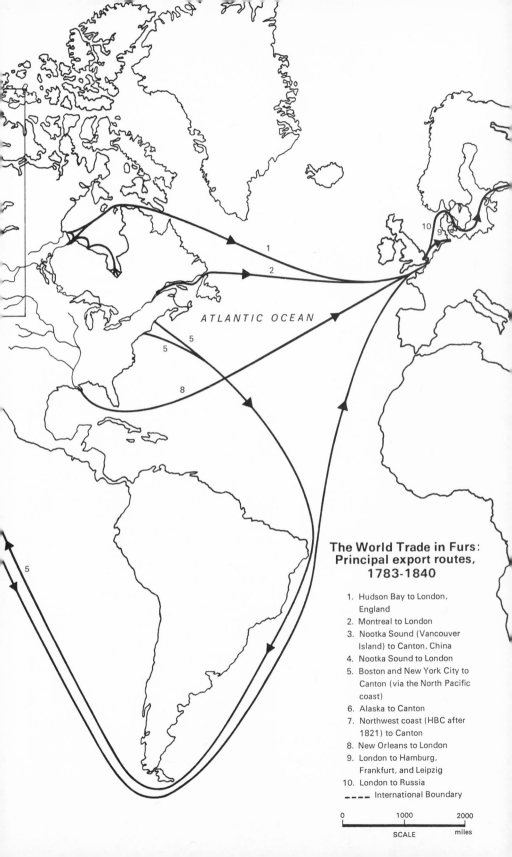

ATLANTIC OCEAN

1

2

5

5

8

5

**The World Trade in Furs:
Principal export routes,
1783-1840**

1. Hudson Bay to London,
   England
2. Montreal to London
3. Nootka Sound (Vancouver
   Island) to Canton, China
4. Nootka Sound to London
5. Boston and New York City to
   Canton (via the North Pacific
   coast)
6. Alaska to Canton
7. Northwest coast (HBC after
   1821) to Canton
8. New Orleans to London
9. London to Hamburg,
   Frankfurt, and Leipzig
10. London to Russia
- - - - International Boundary

10
9

0   1000   2000

SCALE   miles

Introduction

*A*lexander Mackenzie, the trader-explorer who twice led a small group of men through the North American wilderness on extremely difficult, dangerous voyages of discovery, is now a legendary figure. He is honoured as the first man to have reached the Pacific overland north of Mexico, and it is a point of pride to Canadians that his achievement anticipated that of the American explorers, Lewis and Clark, by twelve years. It is common knowledge that Mackenzie published a best-selling account of his travels and adventures, was knighted, and retired to live in his native Scotland. This popular understanding of his life is all the more agreeable and flattering because it seems to be an early Canadian "success" story. The only thing wrong with this assessment is that Alexander Mackenzie's career—including his voyages—was more one of failure than of success.

The popular image of Mackenzie is vague, being little more than that of a courageous man who was a born leader. There is no denying this description. But there was another side to Mackenzie. In his self-confidence there was more than a touch of pride and arrogance. The former is most clearly seen in his private opinion of Indians, whom he nearly always dismissed outright as savages; the latter in his inability to credit colleagues and associates for guidance and help at various points in his career. And his ambition to succeed in life was so great that it generated a streak of ruthlessness that became quite marked with the passage of time and cost him at least two close friendships.

Mackenzie was by no means careless of the feelings of others. He treated Indians firmly but fairly. He always used a blend of sternness and kindness when dealing with his voyageurs, which is the basic reason they served him so loyally and so magnificently. A sensitive man, he hated the crude, isolated existence of the fur trader, which probably explains why at a later time he was so eager to improve the financial lot of those who were junior to him in the trade. Mackenzie could be a very

1

convivial person and had frequent opportunities to demonstrate this after he became a member of Montreal and, later, London society. He relished the pleasures of his day and age: supper parties, private dances, and public balls. In male gatherings he was a cheerful drinking companion, doubtless adding a light touch to the conversation with his dry, sometimes droll, sense of humour. However, it is revealing that while many of Mackenzie's colleagues and associates admired him, they also seem to have distrusted him—his ideas were too bold, his desire to succeed was all too evident.

Mackenzie's biographers have devoted far and away the bulk of their attention to his explorations, and he is therefore remembered today for the two summers that he spent making voyages of discovery to the Arctic and Pacific Oceans. Yet Mackenzie's career spans almost three and a half decades, first as a fur trader, then as a fur-company executive.

This book portrays him as a hardheaded businessman and political visionary as well as the dauntless explorer of history. Relying as it does on Mackenzie's own account and explanation of his life and ambitions in his correspondence and in his book *Voyages from Montreal*, this biography suggests that his explorations were essentially minor episodes in a career largely devoted to reorganizing and unifying the Canadian fur trade. In the process of trying to bring about this reorganization and unification, Mackenzie almost qualifies as a very early father, perhaps a grandfather, of the federation of provinces called Canada.

*   *   *

This biography makes considerable use of Alexander Mackenzie's book *Voyages from Montreal, on the River St. Laurence through the Continent of North America, to the Frozen and Pacific Oceans in the Years 1789 and 1793.* It is only fair to warn the reader at the outset that Mackenzie's authorship has been disputed: several authorities cite the writer as William Combe (1741-1823), an English satirist and a well-known literary hack. While the evidence for this is slight, it seems likely that Combe did have a hand in preparing the *Voyages* for publication. For some years he earned part of his living by restyling the journals of travellers prior to publication. However, this is little more than an interesting footnote to history; Mackenzie was by no means the first celebrity to use the services of a professional writer. The point to note is that Combe had absolutely no personal experience of North America or of the fur trade and would be dependent upon Mackenzie's journals of his voyages. It is clear from the manuscript copy of the account of the voyage to the Arctic—preserved today in the British Museum—that the rewriting done prior to publication was, for the most part, a matter of adding words and phrases from time to time to fill out Mackenzie's lucid, energetic but spare prose. In other words, while the *Voyages* probably owes its occasionally ponderous style to the literary pen of William Combe, the substance definitely reflects the keen eye and practical mind of Alexander Mackenzie.

It has also been suggested or stated by various writers that Mackenzie's cousin, Roderic McKenzie, a fellow fur trader, wrote the book's introductory "A General History of the Fur Trade from Canada to the Northwest." There is no proof that Roderic wrote it. It is true that the two were close friends. For many years Roderic was Alexander's sole confidant, and Mackenzie seems to have regarded his bookish kinsman as a sort of literary confessor. However, considering that the *Voyages* was prepared for publication during a period when the two were barely on speaking terms, it seems unlikely that a man as intensely proud as Alexander Mackenzie would be content to reproduce material written by an ex-friend and business rival. As a matter of fact, although Roderic collected much material on the fur trade during his lifetime with a view to writing a history of the trade, he never did so. The basic point is—as with Combe—that Alexander Mackenzie put his name to the *Voyages* and thus, like any author, must be considered responsible for its content.

In the interests of readability, the spelling and punctuation in the extracts quoted from Mackenzie's writings have been modernized. Quotations from the *Voyages* are from the manuscript on the Arctic voyage and from the 1801 printed text on the Pacific voyage. The sources for the quotations that are not Mackenzie's are listed on pages 182 and 183.

In the map on pages vi and vii, no attempt has been made to locate and identify the hundreds of fur posts that existed—usually for very brief periods of time—in what is now western and northwestern Canada. Despite their grand-sounding names, each of these trading centres was little more than a rather hastily constructed log shack, which was often abandoned after one or more seasons of trading. Another complication is that many a trader built his post literally next to that of a competitor (or on the opposite bank of the same river) and gave his post the same name as that of his rival. In Mackenzie's time western North America contained many fur posts, notably those of the Hudson's Bay and North West Companies but also some maintained by other, smaller concerns or by individual trader-merchants. The map shows only those depots and posts relevant to an understanding of Mackenzie's work and travels.

The Fur Trade

About sixty miles out in the cold, grey waters of the Atlantic from the extreme northwest coast of Scotland is a long, straggling line of islands called the Outer Hebrides. On the largest of these, Lewis, is the small fishing port and Hebridean capital of Stornoway. Here, in 1764, Alexander Mackenzie was born.

Natives of the Hebrides are usually poor. They scratch a bare living from stony soils or dredge it up in fishing nets. But the Mackenzie family was moderately well off, owning both a farm two miles from Stornoway and a house—where Alexander was born—in the town itself. There were four children: Murdoch, who went to sea, and was lost somewhere near Halifax, Alexander, Sybilla, and Margaret.

Practically nothing is known of Mackenzie's boyhood. He himself does not refer to it, and contemporary records offer mere scraps of information. There are, however, two distinct versions of how he came to emigrate to North America and begin his career in the fur trade. One of these implies that he did not get along with his stepmother and says that he left home of his own accord at the age of fifteen, shipping out from Glasgow as a deckhand on a merchant vessel bound for Montreal. This account has a fine romantic ring to it, but the testimony of some of Mackenzie's descendants suggests a quite different story. It seems that his mother died when he was ten years old, and he was taken by his father to New York City to stay with his paternal uncle. The boy had barely settled down in his new home when the American War of Independence (1775-1783) broke out. His father and uncle immediately obtained commissions in a Loyalist regiment. The father died near Kingston, Ontario, in 1780, apparently from an attack of scurvy. The boy was cared for by two aunts, who, concerned for his safety, took him to upper New York State. Sometime later they sent him to stay with friends in Montreal.

This oil painting by Sir Thomas Lawrence, dated about 1800, is the only known likeness of Alexander Mackenzie. It reveals that he was brown-haired, dark-eyed, and with a marked cleft in his chin. Lawrence is considered to have produced sparkling, life-like portraiture rather than the idealized paintings favoured by so many of his contemporaries. Thus it seems that Mackenzie was a striking-looking man who had a strong, bold look to him.

Portrait of Sir Alexander Mackenzie.
The National Gallery of Canada, Ottawa.
Canadian War Memorials Collection.

The first reliable information about Mackenzie's career is that, in 1779, at the age of fifteen, he began to earn his living in the counting-house of Finlay, Gregory & Company, a firm of Montreal fur merchants. In the Preface to his *Voyages*, Mackenzie tells us why he chose this particular business activity.

I was led, at an early period of life, by commercial views to the country north-west of Lake Superior in North America, and being endowed by nature with an inquisitive mind and enterprising spirit, possessing also a constitution and frame of body equal to the most arduous undertakings, and being familiar with toilsome exertions in the prosecution of mercantile pursuits. . . .

In a guarded manner and in rather fulsome prose, Mackenzie admits to seeking his fortune. And this could be done in the fur trade, provided that you were healthy, hardy, industrious, and lucky enough not to be drowned—and if you did not starve or freeze to death.

The five years that Mackenzie spent clerking for Messrs. Finlay and Gregory are a complete blank. The *Voyages* and his correspondence ignore this period, and there is no other known record of these youthful years. As a matter of fact, Mackenzie makes almost as fully-fledged an appearance in history as he does in the *Voyages*—the knowledgeable fur trader and the determined explorer whose discoveries amazed and excited his day and age. In all likelihood, the obscurity of his apprenticeship is explained by the need to learn his occupation. Singlemindedness of purpose and attention to detail were marked characteristics of Mackenzie. Thus he would devote these years in Montreal to acquiring a thorough grasp of the history, geography, and economics of an activity that was as old as the first arrival of Europeans in the Gulf of St. Lawrence.

Doubtless the youth derived his knowledge of the fur trade from several sources, but he probably received a great deal of it from his senior employer, James Finlay. A Scot of some means who came to Montreal shortly after the collapse of the French régime, Finlay had been one of the first British traders from Montreal—perhaps the very first—to venture some two thousand miles to the north and west in 1767 or 1768 and reach that great highway of the northern prairies, the Saskatchewan River. The fact that he was in territory long considered the legal property of the Hudson's Bay Company didn't worry Finlay for a moment. When one or two Company servants he met accused him of trespassing and ordered him out of their employers' lands, Finlay's reply was to offer them employment with him at £25 per year (which was quite a bit more than they were earning) and paid passage to Montreal. He shrewdly gave them his Montreal address and those of his business connections in London in case they should decide to join him at a later date. Finlay was equally confidant and farsighted in his dealings with his customers. He built his trading post deep in Indian country, not far from where the Saskatchewan is formed by the junction of its great northern and southern branches. And those Indians who, initially at least, preferred to canoe down to Hudson Bay and trade their furs there, found some of Finlay's voyageurs waiting for them at two different points farther downriver from his post with canoe-loads of trinkets, muskets, powder, shot, tobacco—and rum. The lesson of Finlay's experiences would not have been lost on Mackenzie: in order to succeed in the trade, you had to be bold.

The late 1760s and early 1770s were pioneer days on the Saskatchewan, when a resourceful man could make a small fortune from just two seasons of fur trading. During the bitter, bloody compaigns of the Seven Years' War (1756-1763) in North America the French, striving desperately to retain a foothold on the continent, had been unable to spare men or money to maintain trade at their western fur posts. Thus there was an extremely profitable market waiting to be exploited when the war ended. European aristocrats and the members of a growing middle class of bankers, merchants, and industrialists had been cut off from a major source of supply of the fur pelts, beaver in particular, from which were made the fashionable felt hats worn by many a lord, gentleman, and navy or army officer—and sometimes by their wives too. And the Indians of the upper Great Lakes region and the Saskatchewan country had been deprived of the European manufactures—axes, chisels, knives, muskets, combs, mirrors, shawls, thread, needles, etc.—which their own

CLERICAL
(Eighteenth Century)

THE CONTINENTAL
Cocked Hat
(1776)

THE WELLINGTON
(1812)

THE PARIS BEAU
(1815)

NAVY
Cocked Hat
(1800)

ARMY
(1837)

THE D'ORSAY
(1820)

THE REGENT
(1825)

The fur trade existed for several centuries because of a persistent fashion in men's hats. Throughout the seventeenth and eighteenth centuries and into the first half of the nineteenth century there was a steady demand in the capitals of Europe for beaver hats, a demand that ultimately became something of a mania. Society, whether royal or aristocratic, clerical or lay, rarely appeared in public without wearing a broad-brimmed beaver hat—plumed, bejewelled, braided or embroidered; high, flat or tricorne in shape according to the fashion of the moment. As can be seen, even army and navy officers wore headgear made from beaver fur. To possess a beaver hat (or hats) was to proclaim one's membership in high society. Like an expensive sports car or a mink coat, it was a status symbol. (It was not uncommon for a man to bequeath his beaver hat quite specifically in his will.) The beaver hat was also a clear indication of wealth. That great seventeenth-century diarist Samuel Pepys records paying £4 for one in a day and age when a much-sought-after architect like Sir Christopher Wren earned all of £200 a year.

Although beaver dominated the fur trade from the beginning, it was not the only furred animal that was trapped. Such pelts as otter, muskrat, ermine, fox, lynx, mink, fisher, and marten were accepted by traders, and even bear and wolf skins had a modest market value.

The beaver hat first became a common headgear among the wealthy in the late sixteenth century. Shortly afterwards, brims were much broadened and hung down noticeably, However, the inconvenience of this wide flapping edge, which was most evident in cavalier times, led to the turning up of first one and then two flaps, until in the very early eighteenth century a third flap was turned up, which ultimately led to the creation of the cocked hat or "Continental." As can be seen, this altered brim remained in fashion in one form or another for many years. And, of course, hats with upturned brims are still common today.

Horace T. Martin, *Castorologia*, Montreal, 1892.

cultures had never produced and to which they had become habituated by many years of commerce with the French. The Indians hungered particularly for firearms and ammunition with which to kill furred animals and for the free (and much diluted) liquor that preceded or accompanied every trading session. At the same time the Hudson's Bay Company, comfortable and complacent in its depots on Hudson and James Bays and accustomed to securing its western supplies of furs from Indians living well north of the Saskatchewan, continued its general policy of enticing these customers to trade at its saltwater posts at Churchill and York Factories. Indeed, it was not until 1774 that the Company built its first post in the western interior, Cumberland House, on an island in the Saskatchewan River.

Of all the traders who ventured into the French fur empire of the West, Mackenzie's employer had been something of an exception. Most traders were financed and outfitted by fur merchants in New York City, Albany, or Montreal, which was destined to become the great focal point of the trade in pelts. Finlay financed his own outfit of three canoes and twelve voyageurs and in his first winter cleared a profit of about £3,000. This capital was used to establish his own company in Montreal. He had been fortunate enough to make a good start, and successive winters spent on the Saskatchewan enabled him to build up a very prosperous operation and enter into partnership with John Gregory, a young English merchant with excellent business connections in London.

The adventurers who bartered for furs in the forests and plains to the north and west of the Great Lakes, a vast stretch of territory that the voyageurs called *le pays d'en haut*, the high or upper country, were of several nationalities. But they shared a common characteristic: a restlessness that drove them to adopt a wilderness way of life. As was often remarked by officials and clergy alike in the days of the French régime, "A trader is a rebel at heart." The fur trade seemed to satisy their need for total freedom and provided them with opportunities to make a great deal of money. A few were French Canadian: the veteran "Franceway" or "Franceways" was working on the Saskatchewan at least three years before Finlay first canoed up that river;

Maurice Blondeau, who had wintered with western Indians as early as 1752, was trading at several prairie posts some years before Finlay first saw the Saskatchewan. Some of these "Pedlars from Montreal," as the men from the Bay contemptuously called them, were from the American colonies, notably a born speculator and handsome huckster called Alexander Henry. Even more hailed from Europe, from England, and, in particular, from the Highlands of Scotland. Mackenzie was destined to meet most of these men and to work with some of them. A handful became notable figures in the history of the trade, specifically as "Nor'Westers"—members of various combinations of Montreal-based fur merchants and western fur traders known to history as the North West Company.*

While a fur trader was essentially an adventurous individual, he had to be tough-fibred and self-sufficient. He had chosen a way of life that exposed him regularly to danger and discomfort—in particular, the threat of starvation and the prison-like confinement imposed by the long, bitter winters of the pays d'en haut.

If a trader was located on the prairies, he could hunt buffalo, deer and game, or simply purchase meat, venison, and fowl from local Indians. Every plains post had a huge *glacière* or icehouse packed each fall with tons of animal carcasses that included buffalo, deer, black bear, swans, geese, and ducks. Yet while buffalo steaks and roasts were satisfying and sustaining, a plains trader was also careful to secure large supplies of the fatty flesh from the animal's hump and back. A mixture of fat and lean meat prevented a man from contracting the sickness that results from a low-fat diet. But in the vast forest belt north of the prairies trading posts had to be built alongside lakes in order to catch fish in great quantities, because there was little to eat but fish all

*In his *Documents Relating to the North West Company*, W. Stewart Wallace has an appendix entitled "A Biographical Dictionary of the Nor'Westers", in which are listed 5 Camerons, 4 Finlays, 7 Frasers, 14 Grants, 5 McDonalds, 5 McDonnells, 4 McDougalls, 8 McGillivrays, 4 McKays, 1 Mackenzie (Alexander) and 14 McKenzies, 7 McLeods, 7 McTavishes, 5 Rosses, 2 Stewarts and 3 Stuarts, in addition to which there were still other Scots named Bannerman, Dowie, Finlayson, Forsyth, etc.

winter long. Of all those caught—whitefish, sturgeon, trout, pike, carp, sucker, bass, and bream, most of which are rich in natural oils—the huge sturgeon of the region was most prized. David Thompson, who spent several winters in the heavily forested country along the Churchill River, described it as the "freshwater hog," adding that "whatever is not required for the day is frozen and laid by in a hoard, and with all care is seldom more than enough for the winter."

There was seldom enough to last out the winter. The threat of famine always menaced the northern posts. There are many records of death from starvation or of traders and voyageurs reduced to roasting bear hides, or eating broths made from beaver skins or from a rock lichen known as *tripe de roche*. In his book, *Travels and Adventures in Canada and the Indian Territories Between the Years 1760 and 1776*, Alexander Henry says that the recipe for the latter was simply a matter of boiling the lichen "into a mucilage, as thick as the white of an egg." It was unappetizing but filling, although eating tripe de roche produced unpleasant side effects. John Long, another trader, remarks that this glutinous mess caused "violent pains in the bowels, and frequently occasions a flux. . . . When the disorder does not terminate in a flux, it occasions violent vomiting, and sometimes spitting of blood, with acute spasms of the bowels."

In fact, almost all a trader's difficulties were the result of living and working in what was essentially a winter country. He spent the brief summer season when the rivers were open transporting furs several hundred miles to a depot—usually Grand Portage on the north shore of Lake Superior or Michilimackinac at the tip of the Michigan peninsula—and then racing back to his post with packs of trade goods before ice put an end to all navigation. For much of the year he had to endure frigid weather with French-speaking voyageurs for company. Next to hunger, his great enemy was boredom. There was little for him to do. Daniel Harmon, a Vermonter who spent twenty years in the pays d'en haut, noted in his diary that "leisure moments" accounted for "nearly nine-tenths" of his time. A trader's duties consisted of little more than extending credit to Indians who occasionally came in to replace a broken musket or buy supplies of ammunition, or entertaining hunters and their families who journeyed to the post to barter furs. If anything, his hardest work was the trading session—dispensing liquor and cheap bribes of combs, mirrors, and beads and then haggling for hours, sometimes days, in order to secure as many furs as possible for the least outlay in goods. Small wonder that a trader often trudged a hundred miles or more through weather that ranged from 30 to 60 degrees below zero to visit another, equally remote, post. Here, he could at least speak English with a compatriot and enjoy with him a few days of reminiscence and gossip, and not a few hours of drunken forgetfulness. These were welcome breaks in an otherwise monotonous, brutish existence that was made even more frustrating by the voyageurs' natural love of the wilderness and their casual, easy relationships with Indians, which few traders could, or even tried to, emulate. It is quite clear from journals and diaries that most traders despised their customers, and many treated their Indian wives or mistresses at best as slaves, at worst as animals.

Among the early adventurers in the pays d'en haut was one whose activities in the Northwest would greatly influence Mackenzie's career. He was a born wanderer from Connecticut called Peter Pond.

Contemporary writers seem to agree that Pond was a loner, and a short-tempered one at that, although he always seemed to get on well with Indians and in his early trading days gained a reputation as a peace maker. He appears to have been a very confident, aggressive man. This is hardly surprising because he was one of a tough breed in a tough business, men who thrived on cutthroat competition and regularly engaged in price wars. Since the great demand in Europe for beaver hats showed no signs of decreasing, in the Great Lakes region in the late 1760s and in the pays d'en haut in the mid-1770s the tempo of competition quickened. The Pedlars from Montreal became steadily greedier in their dealings. Their only concern was to grab up pelts by the hundreds, if not by the thousands. It didn't matter how many Indians were cheated or robbed outright in the process. It was of no consequence whether a trader used liquor, guile, or threats—or all three—provided that he could send canoe-loads of beaver pelts back each summer to his sponsors at Grand Portage, Michilimackinac, Detroit, Albany, or Montreal. And if a man consistently outsold his immediate rivals, he was highly rated, even by those whom he had outsmarted. Pond became a leading member of this unholy fraternity. However, what sets him apart from his commercial brethren is a rather unexpected trait: a desire for knowledge for its own sake. Peter Pond proved to be a self-taught, but talented geographer of considerable achievement.

Pond was a much-travelled man when he canoed into the pays d'en haut in 1775. He had left home at sixteen to join the Connecticut Regiment when the Seven Years' War broke out. He fought as a private in front of Fort Carillon (Ticonderoga), where the French thoroughly thrashed British regulars and colonial militia, served as a sergeant with a force that beseiged and took Fort Niagara, and was present as a commissioned officer at the surrender of Montreal in 1760. Pond had a vague idea of becoming a sailor following his discharge from the army. But after a voyage to the West Indies he returned home to Milford, married, and made a living as a shoemaker for three years—the longest time he spent in one place between the ages of sixteen and sixty. Becoming restless once more, he found employment in the fur trade and worked out of Detroit for some years. Smitten by wanderlust yet again, he made another visit to the West Indies in 1771. Upon his return to Milford he found an invitation awaiting him from an acquaintance in New York City to form a partnership and trade with tribes along upper Mississippi waters. After spending a few years on the upper Mississippi, Pond decided to try his luck north of the Great Lakes, where more—and better—furs were evidently to be had for the taking. Thus, on August 18th, 1775, on the waters of Lake Winnipeg, Alexander Henry noted in his diary that he encountered "Mr. Pond, a trader of some celebrity."

Working on his own, as usual, Pond found his first winter in the plains country just south of the lower Saskatchewan a profitable one. Encouraged by this, the next year he went as far west as the junction of the North and South Saskatchewan Rivers to set up his post. But competition from an aroused

Hudson's Bay Company, which was now sending its servants up the Saskatchewan to build posts on the north branch of the river, cut into Pond's trade. During two successive winters the returns of his labours were much smaller. Having heard vague rumours about fine furs being bought north of the Saskatchewan on the Churchill River, in 1778 he decided to go there and get a share of this business for himself. An added attraction was that the turbulent Churchill, which demanded considerable canoeing skill, was avoided by the men from the Bay, who found it easier to manoeuvre their canoes on the gentler waters of the Saskatchewan.

As it happened, Pond ended up several hundred miles farther north and west of where he had originally intended to go. His plans were changed by the accident of meeting a group of Pedlars who had sensibly decided to try the experiment of joining forces instead of competing among themselves. They pooled their surplus goods and provisions and invited Pond to act as their representative, and trade for furs in a region called Athabasca that was said to be northwest of the headwaters of the Churchill. It was on this river three years before that Alexander Henry, in company with two fellow traders, had intercepted Indians coming down from Athabasca on their way to Hudson Bay. These Chipewyans had long acted as middlemen between the Hudson's Bay Company and other Indians living far to the north and west where winters are eight or nine months long and animal furs correspondingly thick and glossy. Henry and his companions had been amazed by the magnificent quality and quantity of the Athabasca pelts obtained from the Chipewyans. Pond's sponsors were quick to appreciate the importance of Henry's discovery and they wisely picked Pond to advance their interest.

No account by Pond of his epic journey has survived. "The Journal of Peter Pond," preserved today in manuscript form in the Yale University Library, describes only his life as a Great Lakes trader. In 1868, in the kitchen of a Connecticut governor called Pond, a servant was found feeding this manuscript into a stove in the belief that it was waste paper. It is not known how much of the journal was lost in the flames, but the manuscript stops at 1775, the year Pond entered the pays d'en haut. (The principal sources of information about Pond's activities are his maps and their notes.) Mackenzie, who spent an Athabasca winter with him some years later and presumably heard Pond's own retelling, provides the sole contemporary record. In the opening section of the *Voyages* entitled "A General History of the Fur Trade," Mackenzie writes that,

> . . . in the spring of the year 1778, some of the traders on the Saskatchewan River, finding that they had a quantity of goods to spare, agreed to put them into a joint stock, and gave the charge and management of them to Mr. Peter Pond, who, in four canoes, was directed to enter the English River [the Churchill] . . . and proceed still farther, if possible to Athabasca, a country hitherto unknown but from Indian report. In this enterprise he at length succeeded. . . .
>   Here he passed the winter of 1778-9 and saw a vast concourse of the Knisteneaux [Cree] and Chipewyan tribes, who used to carry their furs annually to Churchill . . . they were, therefore, highly gratified by seeing people come to their country to relieve them from such long, toilsome, and dangerous journeys and were immediately reconciled to give an advanced price for the articles necessary to their comfort and convenience. Mr. Pond's reception and success was accordingly beyond his expectation, and he procured twice as many furs as his canoes would carry. . . . Such of the furs as he could not embark, he secured in one of his winter huts, and they were found the following season in the same state in which he left them.

Mackenzie's account of this pioneer expedition into the Northwest is a bare acknowledgement. It is not until much later on in his "General History," when Mackenzie makes his own observations of the route into Athabasca, that one begins to understand something of the difficulties and hazards Pond had to overcome. Mackenzie itemizes them, together with the latitude and longitude of many, and they read like a catalogue of obstacles. There were dozens of portages caused by the wildly plunging cascades and rapids of the Churchill; in numerous places the river races violently through narrow, twisting channels; and its placid stretches of water often concealed masses of tree debris that were close enough to the surface to rip gaping holes in birchbark canoes. Once as far west on the Churchill as Lake Isle-à-la-Crosse (in northwestern Saskatchewan), Pond's route took him northwest over a lake (now named after him) that was "very shallow and navigated with difficulty even by half-laden canoes," says Mackenzie, and shortly afterwards to a place where "the canoes, with their lading, are carried over the Portage la Loche [Methye Portage]." This twelve-mile portage across the height of land that separates waters flowing to Hudson Bay from those flowing to the Arctic Ocean ends in "a very steep precipice, whose ascent and descent appears to be equally impracticable in any way as it consists of a succession of eight hills, some of which are almost perpendicular. . . . "

Once across the punishing Methye Portage and embarked on the Clearwater, a tributary of the Athabasca River, Pond found himself in a landscape completely different from those along the Churchill or Saskatchewan Rivers. He had entered a subarctic region which, with its hundreds of lakes and thousands of square miles of muskeg, is more water than land. It has been aptly remarked of Athabasca that "the country is four-fifths drowned and when not frozen is half-hidden by mosquitoes and black flies." Pond was now at 59°N, almost three thousand miles from Montreal. But as his canoes moved through this desolate, uninviting country, he was looking at the richest fur region the trade would ever know.

The North West Company

*E*ight years passed before Mackenzie joined Pond in Athabasca. The first five were spent in the counting house of Finlay, Gregory, & Company, where he learned the many details involved in importing all manner of trade goods from Britain and exporting to Britain and Europe different types and grades of furs. And it was doubtless during this period when Mackenzie was making daily entries of expenditure and income that he first became concerned by the tremendous costs of maintaining a fur-trade operation from Montreal.

The entire business of bartering for pelts was one that came close to being a form of gambling. Much money was risked and much money was gained, but the chances of bankruptcy were high. A fur company could be ruined by several factors over which it had little or no control: a poor trading season for various inexplicable natural reasons; outbreaks of hostility among native groups (or epidemics of European diseases, to which Indians were very susceptible); adverse fall weather that forced early wintering in overtrapped areas, or particularly violent spring rains and runoff that greatly increased the normal chances of canoes foundering and crews and cargoes being lost. But what came to concern Mackenzie most were two interlocking factors. Slowly but surely during the 1770s, the trade had been reaching farther and farther into the Northwest, and thus it was taking more time and money to transport goods into the interior from Montreal and to bring furs out. However, the whole operation was based on a credit system that became costlier the longer it took to pay off creditors. He explains this last difficulty very clearly in the "General History."

The agents [fur merchants] are obliged to order the necessary goods from England in the month of October, eighteen months before they can leave Montreal, that is, they are not shipped from London until the spring following, when they arrive in Canada in the summer. In the course of the following winter they are made up into such articles as are required for the savages; they are then packed into parcels of ninety-pounds weight each, but cannot be sent from Montreal until the May following so that they do not get to market until the ensuing winter, when they are exchanged for furs, which come to Montreal the next fall and from thence are shipped, chiefly to London, where they are not sold or paid for before the succeeding spring, or even as late as June; which is forty-two months after the goods were ordered in Canada, thirty-six after they had been shipped from England, and twenty-four after they had been forwarded from Montreal. Thus, the merchant, allowing that he has twelve months' credit, does not receive a return to pay for these goods and the necessary expenses attending them, which is about equal to the value of the goods themselves, till two years after they are considered as cash, which makes this a very heavy business.

Longer supply lines to and from the pays d'en haut and rising costs were not the only difficulties. Competition was becoming keener and better organized with the gradual emergence of a strong combination of merchants and traders that did not include Finlay, Gregory and several other small fur firms. Known as the North West Company, it threatened to take over the Athabasca region, the richest source of trade in the pays d'en haut.

Individual trading rivalries, of course, had existed throughout the 1770s. In the latter years of the decade quite a number of Pedlars were competing for the Saskatchewan trade, each man's object being, in Mackenzie's words, "to injure his rival traders in the opinion of the natives." However, every now and again a few Pedlars had enough sense to work together, pooling their goods and agreeing not to undercut each other's prices. This lowered costs and guaranteed each trader a profit. Thus, Alexander Henry joined forces with two of the Frobisher brothers, Joseph and Thomas. This shrewd trio further avoided competition by pushing on north of the Saskatchewan to the Churchill, where they were the only traders on the river. And, as Mackenzie records, it was because of cooperation between

Alexander Henry's (1739-1824) characteristically amiable nature and courtly manners concealed one of the sharpest minds in the North American fur trade. Born and bred in New Jersey, he left home at an early age in search of adventure and money, and found both fairly quickly.

As a sutler with the British forces completing the occupation of New France in 1760, he scented opportunity in a fur trade no longer controlled by the French. He was one of the first men from the English colonies to obtain a trading licence and journey as far west as Fort Michilimackinac (at the tip of the Michigan peninsula), where in 1763 he narrowly escaped being murdered by Indians during Chief Pontiac's uprising. From 1761 to 1774 Henry was a successful trader in the upper Great Lakes region, not least because he entered into partnership with Jean Baptiste Cadotte, or Cadot, a French trader who had great influence among the Lake Superior Ojibwa and, as a result, monopolized their trade in furs.

In 1775, after a costly, futile attempt to make a lot of money quickly by mining surface deposits of copper on the north shore of Lake Superior, Henry decided to recoup his losses by working in the pays d'en haut. He teamed up with the aggressive Frobisher brothers, Thomas and Joseph, and the three of them used liquor and guile to acquire a small fortune in furs on the Churchill River in the spring of 1775. Returning east in 1776 to settle in Montreal, Henry pursued two business careers concurrently: retailing general merchandise and acting as a fur-trade consultant. He sold his interests in the fur trade in 1796, and in later years became, in his own words, "Commission Mercht, Broker & Auctioneer and have a great deal of business."

In 1809 Alexander Henry's Travels and Adventures in Canada and the Indian Territories Between the Years 1760 and 1776 *was published in New York City. (It has been published three times, the latest being a 1969 edition produced by M. G. Hurtig Ltd., Edmonton, Alta.) The book is written in a simple, direct style and is an informative account of exploration and survival in the North American wilderness. Unlike many of his fellow traders, Henry had a considerable interest in and respect for Indians, and thus his diary is a valuable record of native customs, folklore, and cultures.*

Public Archives of Canada.

some traders that Pond was able to reach Athabasca with enough goods to buy a small fortune in furs. Indeed, the rewards of cooperation were plain for all to see. It was, as Alexander Henry observed, "beneficial to the merchants, but not directly so to the Indians, who, having no other place to resort to nearer than Hudson's Bay, or Cumberland House, paid greater prices than if a competition had existed."

This conclusion was also reached by the merchants operating certain Montreal fur firms, particularly when they saw and handled the thick, heavy, lustrous pelts that came from Athabasca. Each was struck by the same thought: with superb furs such as these, a man could make a fortune several times over. The result was a prolonged effort by these men to make Athabasca (and much of the rest of the pays d'en haut) their exclusive territory. They established copartnerships with each other and also with a number of "wintering partners," each firm's senior traders in the pays d'en haut, and used the handy title of the North West Company to describe their common business activities.

The history of the North West Company, which probably began sometime in the middle or late 1770s, is complex not least because its membership was often a changing, usually expanding, one. The name alone is confusing because the organization itself was composed of a number of individual fur companies. However, the North West Company was never at any time in its existence a company in the normal sense of a legally constituted corporation accountable for its actions, financing, etc. It was simply a trading name used by a loose association of men who worked in the same line of business and agreed to turn it into a very profitable livelihood by creating what amounted to a monopoly. Despite its loose nature, from the beginning the Company was an immensely successful combination of experienced wintering partners—Nor'Westers as they proudly called themselves—and a number of well-financed Montreal fur companies.

With few exceptions, Nor'Westers were men who displayed unrelenting opposition to anyone who was not of their number. They acted as if they *owned* the pays d'en haut. Whether competing with traders working for other Montreal companies or with the men from the Bay, they often used Mafia-like tactics— threatening violence, hijacking their competitors' supplies of goods, and bribing, bullying, or intoxicating Indians into becoming their customers. Indeed many Nor'Westers in effect controlled groups of Indians by making them dependent upon handouts of liquor. If these tactics didn't work, their colleagues in Montreal sometimes neutralized competition by bringing rivals into the Company as fellow partners and giving them a share of the profits. These colleagues also handled the Company's public relations. Every fur merchant had to obtain annual government licences in order to trade in the pays d'en haut. Thus the Montreal members were always careful to give officials in Quebec the impression that their wintering associates were an admirable group of trader-explorers who were busy extending the limits of British influence and territory in North America and described themselves as merchants devoted to fostering the flow of furs and goods between Quebec and London. Ruthless, powerful, but outwardly respectable, the North West Company was one of the earliest examples of "Big Business" in North America.

The composition of the Company in 1779, the year in which Mackenzie entered the trade, is curiously interesting. It included a few prominent fur merchants of the time, and Peter Pond is known to have been picked as the group's representative in Athabasca. However, the group also included a Swiss, Jean-Etienne Wadin, *who was both a merchant and a trader, and John Ross, a trader with some experience in the pays d'en haut. At different times, these men ceased to be Nor'Westers, and both died by violence in the pays d'en haut. Some historians and several other writers insist that Pond killed them. Whether or not this is true—and there is room for doubt—the deaths of these men helped to bring about Mackenzie's gradual rise to prominence as a fur trader.

Wadin was the first to die. In 1780 the previous year's agreement among the Nor'Westers was renewed, but it was a revised agreement that left out some of those who had been

*Also found spelled Waden, Wadden, or Waddens.

Thomas, Benjamin, and Joseph Frobisher were a trio of hard-headed, hard-working Yorkshiremen. Little is recorded about Thomas (1744-88) except that he appears to have been the one who took naturally to life in the wilderness. He was one of the early British traders in the pays d'en haut and in 1776 is said to have established the first fur post at Lake Isle-à-la Crosse in what is today northern Saskatchewan. Benjamin (1742-1787) was engaged in the supply end of the trade at least as early as 1765 and was the founder of Frobisher & Company, Montreal, in which his brothers were copartners. However, the career of Joseph (1740-1810), whose portrait this is, completely eclipsed those of his brothers.

The eldest Frobisher had both the audacity of the successful trader and the sagacity of the prosperous fur merchant. He adventured beyond Grand Portage in the late 1760s, always moving on farther west and north when he found competitors catching up with him. In 1774 and 1775 he was on Churchill waters in company with his brother Thomas and in '75 was joined by the enterprising Alexander Henry. This trio had the Churchill trade all to themselves in the spring of that year. Under Joseph's leadership, they used a mixture of cajolery, bluffness, and rum to fleece furs from Chipewyans on their way down to Hudson Bay to trade. And it was on this occasion that the trio learned of the fantastic fur riches of Athabasca.

The details of who organized the North West Company to exploit the Athabasca region are not known, but it seems probable that Joseph had a major hand in the arrangement. He and Benjamin owned two shares in the sixteen-share N. W. Company arrangement of 1779 and were closely associated with two other member firms: (Isaac) Todd & (James) McGill, and (John) McGill & (William) Paterson. In the Nor'Wester reorganization of 1783, the Frobisher firm and Simon McTavish's fur house were major members, holding three shares apiece in a second sixteen-share arrangement. When a further reorganization was necessary in 1787 to absorb Gregory, McLeod, of twenty shares, seven were held by McTavish and Joseph Frobisher (Benjamin died early in 1787). Later that year, the two men merged their businesses to form McTavish, Frobisher & Company, which afterwards became the virtual directorate of the North West Company, determining corporate policy and enjoying a major proportion of each year's profits.

During the period 1787-95, the Nor'Westers encountered little or no opposition in the pays d'en haut and prospered greatly. Joseph Frobisher prospered with them, becoming a very rich man and a highly

influential figure in both official and commercial circles in Quebec. A convivial, genial man, Frobisher was host to many a gathering of notables at his Montreal home, Beaver Hall, a two-storey wooden "cottage" that boasted a frontage of eighty feet and was surrounded by forty acres of land on the southern flank of Mount Royal. And, of course, as one of the founder members of the Beaver Club he was a faithful attender at its often riotous dinner meetings. For some years, he acted as Secretary, and many details of Club business are to be found in Frobisher's manuscript Diary, which covers the period 1806 to 1810 and is preserved today in the McCord Museum, McGill University, Montreal.

members in 1779, one of whom was Wadin. In the winter of 1781/2, Wadin and Peter Pond found themselves forced to spend that season together at a fur post on Lac La Ronge, a large lake in what is now northern Saskatchewan. It is not altogether clear why these two men were both at the same place during the same period. Perhaps this post had become Wadin's regular trading centre. As for Pond, he may have been delayed on his way to Athabasca by early ice conditions on the Churchill River and forced to stop and winter at Lac La Ronge. Whatever the reasons, the result was tragic. According to Mackenzie's "General History," Wadin invited Pond and one of his men, Toussaint LeSieur, to an evening meal. In the course of the evening, Wadin was shot in the thigh, and apparently he bled to death.

The incident is a very mysterious one because there is no evidence as to whether Pond, LeSieur, or possibly a drunken Wadin fired the shot. (Nor is it clear why a tourniquet wasn't used to try and save his life.) And the outcome is equally puzzling. Mackenzie says in the "General History" that "Mr. Pond and the clerk were tried for this murder at Montreal and acquitted: nevertheless their innocence was not so apparent as to extinguish the original suspicion." This is a questionable comment on Mackenzie's part because no evidence of legal proceedings has ever been found, not even in the voluminous correspondence of the contemporary governor of Quebec, Frederick Haldimand, who would have instituted such proceedings had there been a murder trial or a judicial enquiry. There is, dated May 1783, sworn testimony by Joseph Fagniant of Berthier, Quebec, one of Wadin's voyageurs, that his employer was shot in the leg below the knee, although it is clear from the account that Berthier did not witness the shooting. Apparently this testimony was secured by Wadin's widow with the help of a lawyer and forwarded to Governor Haldimand, together with a petition that Pond be tried for murder. And in the Public Archives of Canada is a bill[1] by J. B. Flamand, bailiff of the District of Montreal, dated March 21, 1785, to arrest "toussint LeSieur," summon Joseph Fagniant to attend as witness against Peter Pond and an Antoine LeSieur for murder, and arrest the said Antoine LeSieur. But no record has been found of an enquiry or of a trial.

The entire incident is one of several still unexplained episodes in the history of the trade.

The reaction in Montreal to Wadin's death is not known. Few private records of the fur trade of the eighteenth century appear to have been kept; certainly very few have survived. However, his death may have helped to precipitate a decision in the offices of Finlay, Gregory (for whom Wadin had occasionally worked), because it was about this time that John Gregory made up his mind to contest the Nor'Wester claim to the trade of the pays d'en haut. When Finlay retired in 1783 and sold his interest in the company he had founded, Gregory invited Normand McLeod, a Detroit trader, to become a co-owner. Gregory then hired two experienced western traders, Peter Pangman and the John Ross who had been a Nor'Wester in 1779 and had been excluded from the arrangement of 1783, and also made them partners in Gregory, McLeod & Company. And Alexander Mackenzie became an active associate of these men, a promotion awarded him as a result of a very successful trading mission he undertook somewhere in the Detroit region in 1784. He was offered a partnership in Gregory, McLeod on condition that, like Pangman and Ross, he went to work in the pays d'en haut in the spring of 1785. Apparently he had proved to be a cool-headed, competent trader, able to hold his own against much older, experienced men, and Mackenzie's employers needed his services in their struggle with the Nor'Westers. He accepted the offer and its condition.

One can journey with Mackenzie to Grand Portage, the depot on Lake Superior used by several Montreal companies, simply by reading the early pages of his "General History." However, his keen appreciation of costs causes him to begin by itemizing the contents of each *canot de maître* or freight canoe, basically the Indian birchbark craft, which had been extended and enlarged into a cargo vessel about thirty-six feet in length and six feet in beam. Besides eight or ten men and their baggage, the canoe carried a staggering payload of nearly four tons, composed of

... sixty-five packages of goods, six hundredweight of

The birchbark canoe is a fragile, perishable craft, and of course none has survived from fur-trade days. In 1957 an exact replica of a canot de maître, or Montreal freight canoe, was commissioned by the National Museum of Canada. It was built by Matthew Bernard (at left of unfinished canoe), a former chief of a small band of Algonkian-speaking Indians living on the Golden Lake Reserve, Ontario. These photographs show one stage in construction—fitting ribs into the canoe—and the launching of the finished craft on the waters of Golden Lake.

Although the birchbark canoe was a delicate creation, as easily punctured by a carelessly placed foot as by a submerged rock or tree, it was remarkably waterproof and light in weight. About 75 per cent of the bark of the abundant white or "canoe" birch of eastern Canada consists of water-insoluble waxes, oils, and fats, plus a cork-like layer of suberin. Tough yet pliable spruce roots were used to stitch together the bark frame, and spruce gum mixed and heated with animal fat sealed every seam. The gunwales and thwarts, or crossbars, were made from a high-quality white ash. (One thwart usually had a three-inch hole for a mast.) Cedar ribs formed the flooring and sides of the canoe, and were excellent distributors of the stresses and strains brought to bear on the canoe by wind and wave.

The canoe being launched, modelled after an 1810 canot de maître, is 36 feet, 8 inches in length, 6 feet wide at the centre, and 33 inches deep at the centre. In the trade, this craft was manned by 8 to 14 voyageurs, a bowman or guide, and a steersman. It carried up to 4000 pounds of cargo, provisions, and baggage. The cargo was made up into 90-pound pièces and stowed on narrow poles running the length of the canoe. On occasion, such a canoe could also transport two or three passengers.

National Film Board. Information Canada Photothèque.

biscuit, two hundredweight of pork, and three bushels of pease for the men's provision; two oil-cloths to cover the goods, a sail, etc., an axe, a towing-line, a kettle and a sponge to bail out water, with a quantity of gum, bark, and watape [spruce roots] to repair the vessel. An European, on seeing one of these slender vessels thus laden, heaped up, and sunk with her gunwale within six inches of the water, would think his fate inevitable in such a boat when he reflected on the nature of her voyage; but the [French] Canadians are so expert that few accidents happen.

In addition to cataloguing the rivers and the general location and size of the principal lakes, Mackenzie gives the length in paces of each of the thirty-six portages between Montreal and Grand Portage. He even goes so far as to differentiate between a *décharge*, where the trade goods were carried alongside a river and the empty canoes "lined" or towed upstream, and a *portage*, where both goods and canoes were transported overland. The description of the route is varied now and again by observations on the natural beauty of some particular landscape or remarks about the principal Indian groups occupying the country alongside what has been called "the Voyageurs' Highway."

It soon becomes evident that Mackenzie not only didn't like Indians, to whom he felt vastly superior, but made no attempt to understand their life style and scale of values. Speaking of the Lake of Two Mountains area a few miles west of Montreal, he notes that a Sulpician mission there ministered to about five hundred Algonkian and Iroquois. "So assiduous have their pastors been," he remarks, "that these people have been instructed in reading and writing in their own language and are better instructed than the Canadian inhabitants of the country of the lower ranks; but notwithstanding these advantages . . . they do not advance towards a state of civilization, but retain their ancient habits, language, and customs, and are becoming every day more depraved, indigent, and insignificant. . . . During the winter season, they leave their habitations and pious pastors to follow the chase, according to the custom of their forefathers." This is pretty strong stuff, particularly since it comes from a man who never worked with Algonkians or Iroquois in all the years he spent in the pays d'en haut. One gets the distinct impression that the Indians at Lake of the Two Mountains were not industrious enough to merit his approval.

The only thing missing from Mackenzie's account of the journey to Grand Portage is the human side of it—the sweaty weeks of labour spent by the voyageurs paddling from dawn to dusk in the growing heat of the long summer days and hauling ninety-pound *pièces* or packs of goods over steep, rocky, woodland trails; the violent, seasonal rainstorms that necessitated delays to unpack, dry out, and repack trade goods; the dull but sustaining meals of cornmeal mush mixed with peas and pork fat. And, since it was the height of the insect season, the hordes of mosquitoes and black flies that feasted on exposed flesh, particularly in the course of the overnight halts. It is not until he reaches Grand Portage,* the jumping-off point for the pays d'en haut, that Mackenzie comments on the Herculean labours of his men. From the depot, the pièces had to be hauled uphill over a stony, muddy, nine-mile trail in order to avoid an unnavigable stretch of water where the Pigeon River tumbles down a series of cascades into Lake Superior.

When they are arrived at the Grand Portage, each of them has to carry eight packages of such goods and provisions as are necessary for the interior country. This is a labor which cattle cannot conveniently perform in summer, as both horses and oxen were tried . . . without success.

The fur trade, of course, was utterly dependent upon the canoemen and always had been. Only tough, tireless voyageurs had the strength and stamina to take literally hundreds of tons of goods thousands of miles into the continental interior. Whether they were *mangeurs du lard* (pork eaters) manning a canot de maître between Montreal and Grand Portage, or *hommes du nord* (northmen), the élite canoemen who went into the pays d'en haut in the smaller, lighter *canot du nord*, they were the indispensable

*The portage (and thus the depot) was so named because this was the longest and most difficult carrying-place that the French had encountered.

Mackenzie describes the fur depot of Grand Portage as standing *"beneath an hill, three or four hundred feet in height"* and also remarks that *"the proprietors [wintering partners], clerks, guides, and interpreters mess together, to the number of sometimes an hundred, at several tables in one large hall."* This building stood on a slight rise of ground within the depot and looked out over Lake Superior. Above is a photograph of the Great Hall at Grand Portage as it looked in 1972 after being restored.

About forty miles west along the north shore of Lake Superior from Thunder Bay, Ontario, is Grand Portage National Monument, which is maintained today by the National Park Service of the United States Department of the Interior. Here on the shore of a small bay a few miles west of the international boundary is the site of Grand Portage, *"the Head-Quarters or General Rendezvous for all who commerce in this part of the World"* as a Nor'Wester once wrote. This was a rather exaggerated description of what was little more than a large stockaded post that is said to have contained a total of sixteen well-weathered buildings of cedar and white spruce, the most prominent of which was the mess hall, 30 feet by 95 feet in extent. The other structures were warehouses, dwelling houses, sheds, a counting-house or paymaster's office, a stone-walled, tin-roofed magazine, a cantine where the canoemen spent their wages on food and tobacco or squandered most of their money on liquor, and the pot au beurre or butter-tub as the voyageurs called it, where rowdy or excessively drunken characters were put to cool off.

The original restoration of the Hall burned down in the summer of 1969, which proved to be a blessing in disguise. In the course of excavation on the site of the burned building in 1970, fourteen post moulds were discovered, evidence that confirmed research findings in the late 1960s that the original structure had boasted a long front porch. Excavation also revealed behind the Great Hall traces of a separate building, which may have served as a kitchen. If so, here were prepared the meals that Mackenzie describes as including *"bread, salt pork, beef, hams, fish and venison, butter, peas, Indian corn, potatoes, tea, spirits, wine etc., and plenty of milk, for which purpose several milch cows are constantly kept."*

The term *"Great Hall"* is a modern one given to a structure that contained four bedrooms, used by the Montreal agents during their brief summer residence at the depot, and a large hall 56 feet by 30 feet that was used for purposes other than dining. Here the agents and wintering partners of the North West Company held their annual business meeting each

summer, at which they settled matters of salaries and profits, promotions and appointments, trade policies and plans of expanded activity. Here these same men spent many a night drinking and gambling. And on certain occasions the clerks were invited to attend a formal dance given by their seniors. Daniel Harmon describes one such occasion in his diary:

We had a famous Ball in the Dining Room, and for musick we had the Bag-Pipe, the Violin, the Flute & the Fife . . . at the ball there were a number of this Countries [sic] Ladies, whom I was surprised to find could behave themselves well, and who danced not amiss.

United States Department of the Interior. National Parks Service.

workhorses of the trade. Their basic skill was to take a fragile, heavily laden, birchbark canoe safely through the seething white waters of a *sault* or, more laboriously and equally dangerously, to "line" or haul their craft all the way past it. Their endurance was legendary. It was commonplace for crews to paddle forty strokes to the minute for fifteen hours a day with only two meal breaks in that time and a few short rest spells of ten or fifteen minutes each. They averaged four to six miles an hour in calm waters and, weather permitting, could keep up this pace for weeks on end. Head winds or rough weather brought the risk of swamping and put an end to progress, sometimes for several days. Such was a voyageur's natural impatience with any delay that he described his inactivity as *dégradé*, and "degraded" quickly became part of the vocabulary of English-speaking travellers on the canoe routes of the pays d'en haut. The voyageur was nothing if not vain and never happier than when displaying his strength and dexterity for all to see; many a traveller records his inability to keep up with a canoeman carrying two ninety-pound pièces over a stony portage trail at a steady dogtrot.

To the *engagé*, the salaried voyageur of the fur companies, wind, rain, snow, and sleet were all part of the job. The pay, which varied between £15 and £50 a year, was out of all proportion to his hours of work and the conditions under which he performed them. Yet he thought himself fortunate to receive money and a yearly issue of a blanket, a shirt, a pair of trousers, and a few pounds of twist tobacco. (He received twice as much if he was a northman.) When travelling, he greatly relished the plainest of daily rations: a mush of lyed corn, peas, and pork or bacon fat on the two-month run from Montreal to Grand Portage or, in the pays d'en haut, pemmican in raw chunks or boiled to make what was called "rubaboo." One traveller has left us a pungent description of it.

Rubaboo is a favorite dish with the northern voyageurs, when they can get it. It consists simply of pemmican made into a kind of soup by boiling in water. Flour is added when it can be obtained, and it is generally considered more palatable with a little sugar. Pemmican is supposed by the benighted world outside to consist only of pounded meat and grease; an egregious error; for, from experience on the subject, I am authorized to state that hair, sticks, bark, spruce leaves, stones, sand, etc., enter into its composition, often quite largely.[2]

The voyageur followed a rough, ill-paid, but, above all, dangerous occupation. Canada's lakes are notorious for their sudden summer squalls and storms, which spring up in a matter of minutes and can pound ships, let alone canoes, completely under. On the rivers of the pays d'en haut there were few large saults without tall wooden crosses clustered on the banks to mark the last resting place of an entire crew whose craft had foundered amid jagged rocks and savagely tumbling waters. And alongside stretches of certain prairie waterways a number of crosses bore mute testimony to the effectiveness of Sioux or Blackfoot arrows or lances launched during an ambush. Even the stresses and strains of portaging made hernia a prevalent complaint and not infrequently a cause of death.

In fact, death was always around the next bend of the river or somewhere out on the waters of the lake ahead. But to the breed of man who chose to become a voyageur, his gaiety and pride were such that the presence of death gave added spice to life. The fur trade was an escape from the dull, grinding poverty of rural Quebec and offered him opportunities to see and experience a wider, freer world. A gregarious fellow, he sustained himself with the company of his comrades—and the occasional Indian girl—and his desire to travel to as many places as his employers saw fit to send him. He loved "the forest and the white water, the shadow and the silence, the evening fire, the stories and the singing and a high heart." And if he was picked to become a northman, he regarded this as the finest of compliments and the passport to an even better and more adventurous life. Its reckless satisfactions are clear from the perhaps exaggerated but obviously happy reminiscences of an aged homme du nord, who preferred to live out even his remaining years in the pays d'en haut.

I have now been forty-two years in this country. For twenty-four I was a light canoeman; I required but little sleep, but sometimes got less than required. No portage was too long for me; all portages were alike. My end of the canoe never touched the ground till I saw the end of it. Fifty songs a day were nothing to me. I could carry, walk, and sing with any man I ever saw. During that period I saved the lives of ten Bourgeois [wintering partners], and was always the favorite, because when others stopped to carry at a bad spot, and lost time, I pushed on—over rapids, over cascades, over chutes; all were the same to me. No water, no weather ever stopped the paddle or the song. I have had twelve wives in the country; and was once possessed of fifty horses and six running dogs, trimmed in the first style. I was then like a Bourgeois, rich and happy; no Bourgeois had better-dressed wives than I; no Indian chief finer horses; no white man better harnessed or swifter dogs. I beat all Indians at the race, and no white man ever passed me in the chase. I wanted for nothing; and I spent all my earnings in the enjoyment of pleasure. Five hundred pounds, twice told, have passed through my hands; although I now have not a spare shirt to my back, nor a penny to buy one. Yet, were I young, I should glory in commencing the same career again. I would spend another half century in the same way. There is no life so happy as a voyageur's life; none so independent; no place where a man enjoys so much variety and freedom as in the Indian country. Huzza! huzza! pour le pays sauvage.[3]

At Grand Portage, Mackenzie received orders to take charge of the English (Churchill) River region, establish his headquarters at Lake Ile-à-la Crosse, and oppose Patrick Small, who operated a post there for the Nor'Westers. (Here, Mackenzie first met and became friends with a handsome Highlander called William McGillivray, a Nor'Wester clerk or apprentice trader.) At Ile-à-la-Crosse, Mackenzie was deep in Nor'Wester country and totally on his own. Of his associates, Peter Pangman was stationed quite some distance to the south at Fort des Prairies, a post on the North Saskatchewan River, and John Ross was several hundred miles farther north in Athabasca. The nearest colleague was his cousin, Roderic McKenzie, a clerk recently added to the strength of Gregory, McLeod, who was at Lac des Serpents (Pinehouse Lake) farther down the Churchill.

For the next year or two, the members of the "Little Company," as the Nor'Westers derisively termed Gregory, McLeod, must have offered their competitors a spirited and lively opposition. No details of this period in the trade or in Mackenzie's career have come down to us except for those contained in his comment in the "General History" that

> . . . after the severest struggle ever known in that part of the world, and suffering every oppression which a jealous and rival spirit could instigate; after the murder of one of our partners [in the winter of 1786/7], the laming of another, and the narrow escape of one of our clerks, who received a bullet through his powder horn in the execution of his duty, they [the Nor'Westers] were compelled to allow us a share of the trade . . . this union was, in every respect, a desirable event to us, and was concluded in the month of July 1787.

The murdered man was John Ross. Although it is recorded that the news spread throughout the pays d'en haut that Ross had been killed "in a scuffle with Pond's men," his death has been attributed directly to Pond. Yet, what little evidence there is suggests that it was one or more of Pond's men who slew Ross in the course of a violent argument. Two near contemporaries of Pond—Philip Turnor, a surveyor working for the Hudson's Bay Company, and Peter Fidler, a trader-surveyor in the same organization—both repeat in their individual journals the same account of the murder. One of Pond's men, Péché by name, shot Ross as he was attempting to stop a group of Pond's voyageurs from forcibly taking some Chipewyan customers to their master's post to trade. Fidler adds that, following the killing, Péché sought refuge with the Chipewyans and remained with them for three years before seeking re-employment as a trader. (There is no record that Péché was ever brought to trial or, for that matter, that he was even charged with committing a crime.) And in the Public Archives of Canada is a document[4] entitled

"A report of a special committee of the privy council to consider its powers to try cases of murder in the Indian territory and a number of cases so tried including that of Francois Nadeau and Eustache Le Comte for the murder of John Ross at Arabaska [sic]."

The death of yet another trader did nothing to improve the image of the fur houses in the eyes of the governor and officials in charge of the province of Quebec. Indeed their reaction to the death of a second trader was strongly acrimonious. But the murder of Ross was only one more incident, albeit a brutal one, in the competition between Gregory, McLeod and the Nor'Westers. Officialdom was already angered and alienated by the use of liquor smuggled into the pays d'en haut. For example, in 1785 the "Little Company" had taken 750 gallons of liquor beyond Grand Portage, but their competitors had shipped in 6,000 gallons of rum and 340 gallons of high wine (a concentrated mixture of wine and spirits whose bulk could be doubled, tripled, or even quadrupled by the later addition of water), much of this in kegs that were represented to contain gunpowder, flour, or salt. The resulting debauchery of Indians, who were also being bribed with trade goods, was both vicious and widespread. It was these cynical, widespread practices, which ultimately could neither be kept secret from nor justified to the Quebec authorities, that forced each of the rival groups to recognize the wisdom of acting in unison. And the shock of Ross's death made it impossible to ignore that wisdom. In the summer of 1787, the senior personnel of Gregory, McLeod—including Mackenzie—were made partners in the North West Company.

In his "General History" Mackenzie gives us an inside view of the Company's very simple but very successful financial structure, which had been cleverly organized to offer each member a strong incentive to work as hard as he could. Mackenzie's account explains exactly why the Nor'Westers were such fierce competitors: some partners put up the money to finance the Company's operations, others formed the sales force, but all received a share of the profits. Even the lowly clerks knew that, in time, they would become partners and therefore profit sharers. As Mackenzie points out, the Company was no more than an association of commercial men, agreeing among themselves to carry on the fur trade. . . . It consisted of twenty shares, unequally divided among the persons concerned. Of these, a certain proportion was held by the people who managed the business in Canada, and were styled agents for the Company. Their duty was to import the necessary goods from England, store them at their own expense at Montreal, get them made up into the articles suited to the trade, pack and forward them, and supply the cash that might be wanting for the outfits [clerks' and voyageurs' wages, and the purchase of food supplies], for which they received, independent of the profit on their shares, a commission. . . . The remaining shares were held by the proprietors [traders] who were obliged to winter and manage the business of the concern with the Indians. . . . Some of them, from their long service and influence, held double shares and were allowed to retire from the business at any period of the existing concern with one of these shares, naming any young man in the Company's service to succeed him in the other [by buying the share]. . . . Thus all the young men succeeded in succession to the character and advantages of partners. . . . This regular and equitable mode of providing for the clerks of the Company excited a spirit of emulation in the discharge of their various duties. . . . Indeed, without such a spirit, such a trade could not have become so extended and advantageous, as it has been and now is.

The clerks were paid a salary that varied with length of service and was anywhere from £100 to £400 annually, and they were also supplied with food and clothing. The partners, of course, received their money when the year's annual profit was calculated and then divided by the number of shares. In the period 1790-95, the annual Company profit averaged £72,000 and rose to £98,000 for each of the last four years of the century—and this in a day and age when an income of £1,500-£2,000 a year was considered a comfortable living. Even as late as 1802, when fur-trade rivalries recurred and many of the best fur regions had been practically trapped out, a North West Company share was worth close to £3,300.

In the year in which he became a Nor'Wester,

Alexander Mackenzie was ordered to winter in Athabasca with Peter Pond. The appointment was a considerable compliment, clear recognition of his brief but impressive record as a hardheaded and hard-working trader. The onus of helping to manage the vast, fur-rich Athabasca country would prepare him for even greater Nor'Wester responsibilities in future years.

*M*ackenzie happened to be at Grand Portage in the summer of 1787 when his cousin Roderic and William McGillivray brought the news of Ross's death and he took part in the negotiations that resulted in the partners and clerks of Gregory, McLeod becoming Nor'Westers. As soon as he received orders to winter in Athabasca, Mackenzie ordered his voyageurs to have cargo and canoes ready for him as quickly as possible. His destination was two thousand miles away in the Northwest, and he had to get there with men and supplies before ice on the waters of the pays d'en haut made navigation impossible.

When Mackenzie climbed up the nine-mile portage trail to its western end, he found his hommes du nord patiently waiting for him. Dressed in working clothes of moccasins, deerskin leggings, a breechclout, and a loose shirt or deerhide jerkin, and with their hair hanging down around their shoulders to give them some protection against the millions of insects that infested the north country, they looked like a band of desperadoes. The men squatted or lolled on the ground beside their north canoes, which had been drawn up on the bank of the Pigeon River for his inspection.

Mackenzie thoroughly examined each of the watercraft. He looked inside first to ensure that the wooden frame was sound and that every seam had been freshly caulked with pine gum. He paid particular attention to the birchbark hull. It was maddening to find out after a few hours paddling that some careless canoeman had overlooked a small tear or had done a poor job of patching. (The problem was not repairing a leak, a simple enough task, but wasting precious hours ashore drying out soaked cargo.) Then he examined the condition of the trade goods on the river bank—pièces of general merchandise, bales of tobacco, cases of hardware and firearms, sacks of provisions, and kegs of gunpowder and liquor. Voyageurs were famous for the speed with which they portaged, but they were also notorious for the careless manner in which they handled their loads at each end of a carrying-place. Every bourgeois had to keep a sharp eye open for torn bales and staved kegs, which as often as not proved to be those containing liquor. If he was the least bit lax in checking the routine of portaging or in disciplining the men for carelessness, he was likely to arrive at his post with a large part of the cargo damaged or ruined.

Satisfied by his inspection, Mackenzie gave the order to load up. The canoes were slipped into the water clear of the shallows and held steady by bowman and steersman. Thirty items of cargo were loaded aboard each vessel until there was barely room for each crew to stow themselves and their few belongings.

The brigade of canoes set off up the Pigeon River on one of the worst sections of the journey to Pond's base in Athabasca: six hundred winding miles through the jumbled granite and dense timber of the Precambrian Shield. This was the historic route into the pays d'en haut known as the "Northwest Road." (Fur traders called all canoe routes "roads" and referred to canoe trips as "marches".) The first 150 miles alone involved twenty-nine carrying-places, totalling fifteen miles. One was, according to Mackenzie, "three thousand one hundred paces in length, and over very rough ground, which requires the utmost exertions of the men and frequently lames them." Another, situated between two lakes, was frustrating in a different way, being no more than twenty-five feet long, about the length of a canot du nord. Yet another, the Stairway Portage, was tackled literally by using handholds cut into rock. And everyone in the brigade knew that the last two hundred miles were equally bad—the long length of the Winnipeg River, the "White River" as the voyageurs respectfully called the roaring, tortured waters that necessitated twenty-six portages, whose navigable rapids were awesome enough to make even a northman's heart hammer with fear.

Portages, of course, were only the standard, predictable difficulties on this leg of the journey. The commonest and most infuriating source of delay was the frequency with which head winds, driving high waves before them, swept the larger lakes along the way—Namakam, Rainy, and Lake of the Woods—and brought an end to all canoeing. When this happened, there was nothing to do but pull ashore and stoically endure the hungry attentions of mosquitoes and black flies. In fact, most of the Northwest Road consisted of a series of grey-green lakes. Thus, there were many occasions when brigades were forced to land to avoid waves that threatened to break canoes in two, or to dry out cargo soaked by a heavy rainsquall. But the Road also offered moments of great satisfaction and contentment. On fine days, the lake waters, rimmed with ancient rock and tall trees, glinted and sparkled under a pastel blue sky. Gentle breezes carried from shore the fragrant scent of pine and the rich smell of sun-ripened berries. Moving smoothly through such peaceful surroundings hour after hour, the sun warm on the back and a pipeful of tobacco drawing well, a man forgot the brutal portages and the bloody scourge of voracious insects.

Mackenzie's description of the Northwest Road is as laboriously detailed as that of the canoe route from Montreal to Grand Portage. These sections of the "General History" leave the reader somewhat exhausted, but very aware, as the author intended, of the immense physical difficulties and daily dangers that had to be met and overcome in order to keep Montreal's trade with the interior alive and flourishing. Still, some intriguing glimpses of the past are revealed on this journey. Almost every portage, river, and lake bore a French name, casual legacies left behind by unknown *coureurs de bois** who passed through the region at least a hundred years before the first Pedlar from Montreal crossed the Grand Portage. There is the remarkable rock, still a noted landmark on the shore of Croche Lake, that was smooth-faced but split and cracked in some places. One of the cracks, Mackenzie noted, had a great number of arrows embedded in it, "which is said to have been done by a war party of the Nadowasis or Sieux [Sioux], who had done much mischief in the country and left these weapons as a warning to the Chebois or natives [Chippewa] that, notwithstanding its lakes, rivers, and rocks, it was not inaccessible to their enemies." He was intrigued by the depot at Rainy Lake, whose site is "a beautiful meadow,

*"Runners of the woods," individual fur traders who were refused—or did not bother seeking—the trading licences issued by the government of New France in its attempts to control, and to profit from, the fur trade.

In the summer of 1960, Dr. Edward W. Davis (right), an American mining engineer, with help from D. Richardson (left), a Canadian woodsman, and three scuba divers, carried out some highly successful underwater archaeology. Earlier the same year, Dr. Davis had been idly watching these divers locate a shipwreck off the Minnesota shore of Lake Superior when he was suddenly struck by the idea of getting them to explore the turbulent waterways that fur traders used to journey into the pays d'en haut. If these divers could adjust to the notorious cold and awesome depths of Lake Superior, perhaps they could recover artifacts below rapids and falls where canoes had foundered. Dr. Davis and his helpers quickly found a prize. From a whirlpool below the Horsetail Rapids of the Granite River, about fifty miles from Grand Portage, they recovered a "nest" of 18 graduated kettles. The largest measured 17 inches in diameter and held approximately 7 gallons; the smallest held 3 pints. (Holes in the lugs show where handles could be attached.) They were handmade of hammered brass and have been dated at around 1790.

Since 1960 Canadian and American archaeological teams have been probing rapids and pools along the Voyageurs' Highway. Using such aids as underwater cameras and lighting equipment, and closed-circuit television, they have salvaged an astonishing variety of trade goods: wrought-iron axe heads, flint spearheads, table knives and skinning knives, ice chisels, flintlock muskets and musket balls (about a thousand balls were found below a set of rapids on the Basswood River that even Mackenzie labelled "dangerous"), beads, brass thimbles and buttons—and even a pipe, specially manufactured for the Indian trade, with burned, caked tobacco still in the bottom of the bowl.

Minnesota Historical Society.

surrounded with groves of oaks . . . also the residence of the first chief, or Sachem, of all the Algonquin tribes inhabiting the different parts of this country. . . . Here also the elders meet in council to treat of peace or war." But, characteristically, there is the sanctimonious comment that the Indians who inhabited the region could live very comfortably on its abundance of fish and game were they not "immoderately fond of spirituous liquors."

When he arrived at the mouth of the Winnipeg River, Mackenzie's route took him over the shallow, wind-tossed waters of Lake Winnipeg to its northwestern corner, where the Saskatchewan River has its exit. Inevitably there was a long portage, Grand Rapids,* near its mouth. Then his brigade had to thread a careful way through the snake-like, marshy channels of the river's delta, the lead guide anxiously watching out for the constantly shifting mud banks just under the water's surface. It took several days to pass through this swampy region, and everyone felt a deep sense of relief when they had left behind the evil-smelling mists and clouds of insects that hovered over the waters of the lower Saskatchewan. Moving briskly upriver, the brigade soon caught sight of Cumberland House, the great inland depot of their rivals, the men from the Bay. Here, Mackenzie and his men swung north to reach Churchill waters via the steep rapids of the Sturgeon-Weir River, which northmen always referred to with marked bitterness as "La Rivière Maligne."

Some of Mackenzie's observations on the southern approaches to Athabasca are remarkably graphic and form one of the few accounts that, even today, we have of this region of Canada. He describes the Churchill as a staircase-like succession of lakes rather than a normal waterway, and his explanations of some place names are fascinating historical sidelights. As he crosses the Portage du Traité leading from Saskatchewan to Churchill waters, he observes that the carrying-place was once known as Frog Portage. Years, before, when the Cree gradually moved west in search of more beaver pelts for the Hudson's Bay Company, they encountered bands of Chipewyans, whom they considered less skilled than themselves in hunting beaver and preparing the skins. As a sign of derision, the Cree stretched the

*Now submerged beneath the waters of a storage lake created by a power dam.

skin of a frog and hung it up at this carrying-place. The Portage des Morts on Churchill waters is another example. This was a point of land covered with human bones, relics of the smallpox epidemic of 1780/81 that swept through the tribes of the West "as the fire consumes the dry grass of the field". And far up the Churchill, as he traversed Lake Isle-à-la-Crosse, Mackenzie notes that this body of water got its name from "the game of the cross [lacrosse], which forms a principal amusement among the natives."

About fifty miles north of Isle-à-la-Crosse, Mackenzie came to the height of land separating waters draining down to Hudson Bay from those running to the Arctic Ocean. The divide was crossed by the Methye Portage, a twelve-mile trail over a low, sandy ridge that drops steeply down seven hundred feet at its northern end, the worst portage known to fur traders at this time. But Mackenzie did not take his brigade over the trail into Athabasca. Although it was only early October, just short of the Methye Portage he had found running water frozen over, a sure sign of an early winter. Freeze-up comes with incredible swiftness in the north country. At any time of day or night the thinnest film of ice on a waterway can become, within minutes, an opaque, rapidly thickening crust. He therefore cached his merchandise at the north end of the carrying-place, left most of his men to build winter quarters at a lake south of the portage, and pushed on as quickly as possible with eight canoemen. Although occasional mild spells broke up the ice on the Athabasca River from time to time, the blizzards and severe cold spells that herald the onset of the northern winter were such that it took Mackenzie and his party almost the rest of the month to march to the safety of Pond's headquarters.

Pond's base was far from imposing. A few log huts, clustered together near the Athabasca River, occupied a tiny clearing in the vast, dark northern forest of jack pine, spruce, and white birch. The post seemed no different from dozens of others in the pays d'en haut. But there was one significant difference. The location had been very carefully chosen: Pond's base was as deep in the Northwest as was practicable. Athabasca fur brigades had only five months between break-up and freeze-up to canoe and portage all the way down to and back from their special supply depot at Rainy Lake House (several hundred miles north-west of Grand Portage) before the formation of river ice halted all progress. A fast-moving river such as the Athabasca usually broke up late in May, a month earlier than the huge lake into which it emptied. These four weeks made all the difference between the brigades retracing the fifteen hundred miles from Rainy Lake House or being forced to winter somewhere along the Churchill. In addition, the nearby delta of the Athabasca provided fish in abundance to maintain the fort's inhabitants through the long, savage northern winter. Eating was one way of combatting the subzero temperatures, although as a seven-teenth-century French explorer remarked half proudly, half ruefully, "To withstand the cold [of the north country], one ought to have his Blood compos'd of Brandy, his Body of Brass, and his Eyes of Glass."

Roughly three-quarters of the way through the "General History" Mackenzie ends his journey to Athabasca, remarking that Pond's post, "The Old Establishment," was built in 1778/9 about forty miles upriver from the lake. From this point on there is only one brief mention of Peter Pond. This is an amazing omission because there was no one else who could have given Mackenzie the geographical data, rough as it was, on which he was to base both his day-to-day operation of Company affairs in Athabasca and his own explorations. No one else in the trade had collected such a mass of geographical facts and speculations, largely because of a desire to solve the geographic problem that had fascinated trader-explorers since the time of Champlain: a water route to the "Western Sea," the Pacific Ocean. Yet Mackenzie does not spare so much as a single line to credit Pond's many attempts to resolve this puzzle. There is much truth in the old adage that jealousy has always been the explorer's sin.

We will never know exactly why Mackenzie ignores Pond and his achievements. Neither the "General History" nor his correspondence offers any definite information, and contem-porary writers do not comment on relations between the two. But it is not hard to make a few guesses. As indicated earlier, Pond does not seem to have been an amiable man. And he must have been soured by the knowledge that after twenty-six years in the trade, of which fourteen had been spent in the western interior, he still held only one share in a company in which his colleague, with only three winters' experience to his credit, also possessed a share. In short, Pond would not be the easiest of companions with whom to share the confined life of a fur post in winter. As for Mackenzie, he had more than his share of pride. He seems to have been convinced that he made his way in the trade without help from anyone; the "General History" gives no other impression. There is nothing in it of the apprentice. The image is that of the knowledgeable historian* and the successful wintering partner. And in the two journal sections that follow the "General History" and detail his voyages of 1789 and 1793, there is the further image of the dauntless explorer. Indeed, various incidents in Mackenzie's life strongly suggest that arrogance was a major trait. This overweening pride, together with the suspicion that Pond had had some hand or other in the deaths of Jean-Etienne Wadin and John Ross, would hardly recommend Pond to Mackenzie.

Despite Pond's uncertain temper and Mackenzie's reservations about his colleague's character, the two men probably managed to get along together. This seems clear from a comment that Mackenzie included in a letter to his cousin, Roderic, towards the end of 1787: "This far my neighbour and I have agreed very well and I believe we shall continue on the same good footing for the season." His comment is not altogether surprising. The young Scot and the aging Yankee were curiously alike. Each was a confident, strong-minded personality. Each had been remarkably successful in a trade that rewarded audacity and authority. Lastly, and perhaps most importantly of all, although

---

*Mackenzie is not altogether reliable as a chronicler of the trade, as the following examples illustrate. It has been clearly established by several historians that his account of Wadin's death is wrongly dated: Wadin died, not in March 1781 as Mackenzie reports, but a full twelve months later. As already noted, Mackenzie remarks that Pond and his clerk were acquitted of any responsibility for Wadin's death, but there is no confirmation in official files that a trial or an enquiry was ever held. At one point in the "General History", Mackenzie implies that the North West Company was founded in the course of the winter of 1783/4, yet there are records confirming that it existed at least as early as 1779.

the reason for his interest was a quite different one, Mackenzie came to share Pond's consuming desire to solve the mysterious geography of the lands north and west of Athabasca.

During the winter of 1787/8 Pond would explain to Mackenzie the wide-ranging operations of the Athabasca Department of the North West Company. It had all begun nine years before when Pond had found his way into Athabasca via the Methye Portage and gradually established a network of posts at which highly successful trading operations were conducted with several Athabaskan-speaking tribes—Beaver, Chipewyan, Slave, Dogrib, and Yellowknife. Pond had discovered that the tributaries and backwaters of the region's two great waterways, which the Indians called the Athabasca and Peace Rivers, were breeding grounds for countless millions of fur-bearing animals and natural highways for his men to contact Indians along these rivers. He had found more customers north of Lake Athabasca living beside an extension of the Peace River called the Slave River and also along the shores of another huge body of water, Great Slave Lake, each area being a source of magnificent pelts. But in all likelihood Pond spent far more time talking about the geography of the Northwest, his favourite subject.

Sometime in the 1780s Pond had become preoccupied with charting the rivers, mountains, and ultimate boundaries of the regions beyond his post. He may have been stimulated by Indian reports that Russian fur traders had established a trading post somewhere on the Pacific coast of North America. In any case, Pond was extremely curious about the Pacific Ocean. How did one reach it overland? What routes led to it? And how did the Arctic Ocean fit into the topography of the Northwest? Was it true, as Indians told him, that there was a mighty river north of Lakes Athabasca and Great Slave that ran down to a frozen sea? Was this the water route to the Pacific, perhaps via the legendary Northwest Passage? His basic difficulty, of course, was the one that had plagued explorers since the time of Samuel de Champlain: when responding to questions, Indians were eager to please and usually gave the kind of positive—but misleading—answers that they thought were wanted.

Pond spent many an Athabasca night trying to piece

together the jumbled mixture of what he knew and what he was told, much of which was vague and conflicting in nature. (It is not clear how much of the Athabasca region Pond actually explored, but it seems that he may have got as far north as Great Slave Lake.) Eventually he managed to work out for himself one key fact of the geography of the Northwest. The Athabasca River, which flowed past his post, and the even larger Peace River that his informants said "descended from the Stony or Rocky Mountains" form the forked tail of a mighty water system that drains down to salt water.

By March 1784, with information obtained from Indians and even from his traders and their voyageurs, Pond had completed his first two maps of the Northwest.* They are obviously the work of an amateur cartographer, for the accuracy of their latitudinal and longitudinal markings leaves much to be desired. Pond's locations of certain lakes are simply wishful thinking; some are complete inventions. But the maps show, with remarkable accuracy, the principal rivers and bodies of water north and northwest of the Great Lakes. And Pond must have carefully sifted the information he garnered because he clearly identifies several important natural features. He indicates that the Athabasca River rises on the east side of the Rocky Mountains—which it does. The "Stony Mounts" themselves appear as an unbroken barrier in the west, except for a single waterway flowing eastward that pierces them in the latitude of 61°N—which is exactly what the Peace River does in the latitude of 56°N in the course of its journey down into what we call the Mackenzie drainage basin. As a matter of fact, the Peace is the only river that breaches the Rockies, a mountain chain that, as Pond correctly indicates, reaches as far south as northern New Mexico. Pond also shows a water route from Lake Athabasca to Great Slave Lake and thence to a "mer du Nord West" or "Ice Sea" that he describes in his map notes as tidal water—which is exactly the main drainage pattern of the Mackenzie basin. (The river marked on modern maps as the Mackenzie is the waterway

*So far, none of Pond's original maps have been found. Several have survived that are presumed to be genuine copies of his originals.

The trading store in a fur post was not unlike a modern corner grocery: it stocked everything from basic necessities to the occasional luxury item. At the counter at the far end, Indians and their wives bartered pelts for salt, sugar, soap, tea, kettles, pots and pans, bags of a brilliant pigment known as vermilion (which was used to paint faces, bodies, and robes), bolts of cloth, muskets and gun flints—and jugs of liquor.

In this store, reconstructed as part of a special exhibit at the Centennial Museum in Vancouver, two highly-priced items have been given their usual prominence. The loaf-like items hanging from the overhead strings are carrottes *of leaf tobacco, carefully rolled in linen and securely tied with cord. Obvious eyecatchers are the Assomption sashes, the red or crimson, usually arrow-patterned,* ceintures fléchées. *(The name derives from L'Assomption, Quebec, where the finest sashes were woven.) Any Indian fortunate enough to possess one was able to give an added touch of elegance to even the finest buckskin garments.*

Vancouver Centennial Museum, Vancouver, B. C.

flowing some eleven hundred miles from Great Slave Lake to the Arctic Ocean.)

Pond had presented one of these maps to the Congress of the newly-established republic of the United States in the course of a brief visit to New York City in March 1785. Upon his return to Quebec the following month, he presented the second, more heavily annotated map to the governor of Quebec. Presumably Pond was seeking government support for, or approval of, trading-cum-exploring activities and was trying to get American or British officials (or both) to aid these activities, although there is no evidence that officialdom gave his maps anything other than polite attention. However, while talking with associates in Quebec later on in 1785, he heard of Captain James Cook's epic voyage of 1776 to 1779, the primary purpose of which was to find the Pacific gateway of the fabled Northwest Passage. After Pond had acquired and studied a copy of the great navigator's text and maps of the voyage, he lost all interest in the "Sea of the Northwest" as a possible route to the Pacific.

Cook's descriptions of the lustrous beauty of the sea otter's pelt and the abundant numbers of this Pacific-coast cousin of the beaver were exciting. And Pond had been too long a trader not to be attracted by the fantastic prices for which sea otter pelts were sold in the great Chinese port of Canton, both by Cook's crew and by Russian traders working on the North Pacific coast. The wealthy Chinese mandarin class prized the fur of the sea otter highly as muffs, caps, or trimming for their robes and willingly paid considerable sums of money to indulge their taste, the more so since the sea otter's fur is perhaps the finest and hardest-wearing of all animal pelts. But Pond was much more attracted by what the explorer had seen at one particular location on the north Pacific coast, Cook had found a large estuary that he thought might be "a strait communicating with the northern seas," but it narrowed and "the marks of a river displayed themselves," thick, muddy water "very considerably fresher than any we had hitherto tasted" and full of "large trees and all manner of dirt and rubbish." This estuary, now known as Cook Inlet, has at its eastern end (near the site of modern Anchorage, Alaska) a complex of minor waterways that the great navigator took to be "a great river," which was later officially named "Cook's River" in his honour. To Pond, this suggested the exit of a huge waterway that either flowed through or originated in the Athabasca country to the north of his post. But he was deceiving himself very badly. Pond was never able to cope with the mathematics of longitude; as a result he always assumed that the Pacific was just a few days' canoeing directly west of Lake Athabasca.

The possibility of a direct water route from Athabasca to the Pacific obsessed Pond. The more he queried Indians about the river exiting from Great Slave Lake—and the Mackenzie does, initially, flow westward from Great Slave—and the more he studied Cook's text and maps, the more he convinced himself that it led, not to the Arctic as he had first supposed, but to the Pacific. He calculated this waterway to be in the neighbourhood of 64°N, and Cook's text and maps described the outflow of "a great river" at 61°N.

The result of Pond's theorizing was a map of the Northwest dated 1787, which incorporated Cook's discovery of the southern and western coasts of Alaska and an island string (the Aleutians) leading out into the Pacific. Clearly identified on the map are Great Slave Lake and an immense waterway flowing westward from it that ends abruptly in the middle of nowhere— and a large river, marked "Cook's River," that begins equally abruptly in that same stretch of unknown territory and is shown flowing into Cook Inlet. The implication is obvious. To Pond, these were one and the same waterway. Unfortunately, like many men before and after him, Pond was bending facts to fit a theory. There is no water connection between Great Slave Lake and the Pacific. He was right the first time: the waters of the lake flow to the Arctic.

It only remained to prove by exploration that "Cook's River" did lead to and from the Pacific, and Pond seems to have planned to do this. But in the spring of 1788 he handed over the Athabasca Department to Mackenzie and left the Northwest forever.

It is not clear why Pond made this decision. We know so little about individual eighteenth-century fur traders that ninety-nine times out of a hundred we have to guess at the motives of even the more famous among them. Perhaps Pond was conscious of his age and failing physical powers. He was now close to fifty, and few men were able to sustain the hardships of the trade much beyond the age of forty. Indeed, many a wintering partner was in poor health by the time he had reached his middle thirties. On the other hand, this decision may have been forced on Pond. According to some historians he was deeply angered that the Company had made no provision for him other than a single share and decided to seek employment in the United States; others suggest that his Nor'Wester colleagues, embarrassed by the violent incidents in his life, induced Pond to give up his wintering duties. It has also been suggested that his colleagues wished to use Pond to influence Quebec authorities into giving the Company a monopoly of trade as a reward for his contributions to geographical knowledge. Whatever the reason, it is recorded that he sold his single share in the North West Company to William McGillivray for £800 and severed his connection with the organization.

After spending some time in Montreal and Quebec City with various associates, Pond returned to Milford, Connecticut. We catch a few glimpses of him thereafter. In 1790 he called upon Ezra Stiles, the President of Yale College, and chatted at some length about his explorations. Early in 1792 he was appointed a special U. S. Government agent to the Indians in the Detroit area. Some time around 1800 Pond began to write his memoirs. The next information we have is his death (1807) in his native Milford, apparently in circumstances of poverty. One of the few charitable comments on Pond's life is from the pen of Mackenzie's cousin, Roderic, who wrote, "He thought himself a philosopher and was odd in his manners."

The year that Pond left the pays d'en haut Mackenzie had his cousin Roderic officially transferred to his department to supervise the construction of a large trading centre on the southern shore of Lake Athabasca. Trade with Athabascan tribes was steadily increasing, and Fort Chipewyan,* as it was called, was

---

*This was the first Fort Chipewyan, constructed on a point of land eight miles east of the entry of the Athabasca River into the lake. At a later date a new Fort Chipewyan was built on the northwest shore.

a much more central location for many customers than Pond's post.

Mackenzie seems to have had some difficulty persuading his cousin to accept the approved transfer. Roderic had long been disgusted by the sordid, mercenary nature of the trade and was on the point of quitting to seek some other livelihood in Montreal or Quebec City. His kinsman had failed several times to convince him that the financial rewards of a partnership would make up for much of the drudgery—"slavery" as Roderic termed it—of a clerk's life in the pays d'en haut. Finally, Roderic was persuaded to remain in the trade. Apparently, Alexander mentioned the likelihood of his going off exploring and begged his cousin to be prepared to run the department in his absence.

Several writers have assumed that when Mackenzie went exploring he did so solely on his own initiative. This is highly unlikely, and the matter is discussed at some length in Chapter Seven. So far as the journey to the Arctic is concerned, it will suffice for the moment to point out that three pieces of writing, two of them letters, cast considerable doubt on the assumption that Mackenzie simply took over Pond's work of exploration and, on his own, carried it forward.

There are several references in Pond's cartographic notes on maps dated July and December, 1787, to indicate that he was preparing these to present to Catherine the Great of Russia, some of whose subjects were doing a very nice trade in sea-otter skins up and down the coast of the Pacific Northwest. While in Quebec in October or November, 1789, Pond had several conversations about the Northwest with Isaac Ogden, a Loyalist from New Jersey and, at this time, a judge of the Admiralty Court at Quebec. In a long letter, Ogden wrote the substance of those conversations to his father in London. Among other things, Isaac Ogden remarks,

> Another man by the name of McKenzie was left by Pond at Slave Lake with orders to go down the River ["Cook's River"], and from thence to Unalaska [a Russian fur post], and so to Kamskatsha [the Kamchatka Peninsula of Asiatic Russia], and then to England through Russia. If he meets with no accident, you may have him with you next year.[5]

The second letter is one of Mackenzie's. In February 1789, almost four months before setting off on the exploration that took him all the way to the Arctic, he wrote the agents of the Company a general report on operations in the Athabasca Department. In the last paragraph is the statement, "Should I not go out in Spring and should you mean to send anyone to take charge of this department in case of accident, Roderic Mackenzie if he will undertake it will, from his experience and local knowledge, be in my opinion the fittest person you can find." Mackenzie can only be referring to the possibility of his *not* attending, as he usually did, the annual meeting of the Montreal agents and the wintering partners each summer at Grand Portage and the possibility of his being absent from the Department in the summer of 1789. He was not due for a year's leave of absence from the pays d'en haut, a leave normally granted wintering partners every six or seven years. So where else would he be going except on exploration?

The third piece of writing is the very title of the journal of the voyage to the Arctic. The manuscript of the 1789 expedition, the only part of the *Voyages from Montreal* where Mackenzie's writing is clearly separable from William Combe's additions, is entitled "Journal of a Voyage performed by Order of the N. W. Company, in a Bark Canoe in search of a Passage by Water through the N. W. Continent of America from Athabasca to the Pacific Ocean in Summer 1789." In the *Voyages from Montreal*, there is no mention of "by Order of the N. W. Company." The title is simply "Journal of a Voyage, &c."

It is important to note that Mackenzie set out in June 1789 to reach the Pacific overland. The Preface to the *Voyages from Montreal* implies that his object was to prove or disprove the existence of the fabled Northwest Passage from Europe to Asia. Mackenzie remarks:

> The first voyage has settled the dubious point of a practicable North-West Passage; and I trust it has set that long agitated question at rest and extinguished the disputes respecting it for ever.

This was certainly the result of the voyage and is unarguable, but his *intent* was something quite different. In the manuscript of his journal account of the first voyage, he remarked near the end of the outward leg that

> . . . my going farther in this direction [north] will not answer the purpose of which the voyage was intended, as it is evident these waters must empty themselves into the Northern Ocean

The purpose of the voyage is clearly stated in a memorandum appended to the manuscript:

> . . . It was in the summer of 1789 that I went this expedition in hopes of getting into Cook's River; tho' I was disappointed in this, it proved without a doubt that there is not a North West passage below this latitude [69 15′N], and I believe it will generally be allowed that no passage is practicable in a higher latitude, the sea being eternally covered with ice.

Mackenzie tailored his book for public consumption, preferring to emphasize the discovery that there was no northwest passage through the continent rather than admit that his venture was unsuccessful because it was based on someone else's theorizing. He admitted his intent as early as November 1794, when he reported in writing to Lord Dorchester, Governor General and Commander-in-Chief of British North America, that

> I followed the course of the waters which had been reported by Mr. Pond to fall into Cook's River; they led me to the Northern Ocean, in latitude 69 1/2° North and about 135 of West Longitude. . . . It proved that Mr. Pond's assertion was nothing but conjecture, and that a North West passage is impracticable.

The personal motive behind Mackenzie's two explorations was a strongly economic one. He wanted to find a navigable waterway to the Pacific coast so that trade goods and furs could be freighted *in bulk* between Europe and the Northwest instead of being hauled at great expense in ninety-pound pièces over the many miles of wilderness waters between Montreal and Grand Portage and between that depot and all the interior posts. Long before most of his compatriots did, Mackenzie clearly saw that a cheap supply route by sea was the basic strength of the Hudson's Bay Company, together with the fact that the main depots on the Bay—Churchill Factory and York Factory—were farther north and west than Grand Portage. His years in the counting house in Montreal had shown him that fur trading was financed by borrowing enormous amounts of capital in the form of trade goods. His early years in the interior convinced him how dangerous—if not insane—it was to expose this capital to the vagaries of rock and rapid. As he stresses in the *Voyages from Montreal*, transport to and from the most distant parts of Athabasca

> . . . occupies an extent of from three to four thousand miles through upwards of sixty large lakes and numerous rivers and the means of transport are slight bark canoes. It must also be observed that these waters are intercepted by more than two hundred rapids, along which the articles of merchandise are chiefly carried on men's backs and over an hundred and thirty carrying-places, from twenty-five paces to thirteen miles in length, where the canoes and cargoes proceed by the same toilsome and perilous operations.

This fantastically long, fantastically expensive transport route—to which must be added another three thousand-mile haul of goods from and furs to Britain—was the reason why the margin of profit over cost was never very great for the Montreal fur trade. In fact, Mackenzie estimated that the cost of transportation was one half of the total cost of carrying on the trade. It is true that a few men made fortunes in the trade but only, as Hugh MacLennan has remarked, "by penny pinching and a driving of the voyageurs to a degree which would horrify a modern trade union."

Mackenzie, an exceedingly profit-minded Scot, was determined to lessen the tremendous imbalance between expenditure and income in the Northwest trade. His first attempt to do so was his voyage of 1789.

The First Exploration, 1789

*M*ackenzie's account of his first voyage begins in typically matter-of-fact fashion: "Wednesday, June 3. At 9 o'clock embarked at Fort Chipewyan. Mr. Leroux with canoe for Slave Lake in company." Thanks to William Combe, we learn that the explorer shared his canoe with four French Canadians, two of whom had brought their Indian wives along, and a German. An Indian, who had acquired the title of English Chief, and his two wives travelled in a separate, smaller canoe; and a couple of young Indians, followers of the chief, accompanied the party in a third birchbark craft.

The Canadians were Joseph Landry, Charles Ducette, François Barrieau, and Pierre de Lorme. That a German should seek employment as a voyageur is very intriguing, but there is no explanation as to why John Steinbruck was working for the North West Company. The Indian with two wives was, Combe notes,

> . . . one of the followers of the chief[Matonabbee] who conducted Mr. Hearne [Samuel Hearne of the Hudson's Bay Company] to the Coppermine River and had since been a principal leader of his countrymen who were in the habit of carrying furs to Churchill Factory, Hudson's Bay, and till of late very much attached to the interest of that company.

As a result, this Chipewyan was always known as English Chief. Laurent Le Roux, or Leroux, who had entered the trade as a clerk in the service of Gregory, McLeod & Company, became a Nor'Wester when his employers became part of the North West Company in 1787. He had been a leading Athabasca trader under Pond and was one of Mackenzie's senior men.

Mackenzie had supervised the contruction of his own canoe. It was thirty-two feet long and designed to carry twenty-five pièces of goods, a few bags of pemmican and of corn as emergency rations, and a crew of four and their gear. In addition to the customary iron-shod punting poles, and towing lines, each of the watercraft was provided with a mast and a sail of double-sewn canvas. Mackenzie personally checked the quantity and quality of the repair materials being taken along: the watape* (spruce roots used as twine to sew up rips in the bark of the canoes), and the containers of pine gum to seal leaks. He paid particular attention to the cloths soaked in oil and animal fat that were the makeshift waterproofing laid over the cargoes of trade goods. Then he doublechecked that the canoes carried the spare muskets and extra shot and powder he had ordered. Mackenzie was taking off into the unknown and, characteristically, was going to be prepared for all possible contingencies.

The first day's run was only thirty-eight miles around the western end of Lake Athabasca to where it empties into a waterway known as the Rivière des Rochers—enough mileage to get the expedition under way and to loosen up the canoemens' muscles. From this point on, the day's travel would begin at four in the morning and extend until seven in the evening. The speed of progress would seldom be less than four miles an hour and would often be eight or ten. A contemporary account by a young army officer makes it quite clear why a canoeman had to be fed as much as eight pounds of food daily when "on the march."

No men in the world are more severely worked than these Canadian voyageurs. I have known them to work in a canoe twenty hours out of twenty-four, and go at that rate during a fortnight or three weeks without a day of rest or a diminution of labour; but it is not with impunity that they so exert themselves; they lose much flesh in the performance of such journeys, though the amount of food they consume is incredible. They smoke almost incessantly, and sing peculiar songs, which are the same their fathers and grandfathers and probably their great-grandfathers sang before them; the time is about the same as that of our quick military marches, and

*Mackenzie describes it as the divided roots of the spruce, which the Indians "weave into a degree of compactness that renders it capable of containing a fluid. Different parts of the bark canoes are also sewed together with this kind of filament."

is marked by the movements of their paddles. They rest from five to ten minutes every two hours, when they refill their pipes; it is more common for them to describe distances by so many pipes, than in any other way.[6]

On each of his voyages Mackenzie hoarded his supplies of pemmican and corn and fed his party off the country-side as much as possible. Thus, as soon as the party had landed for the night, he and his hunters usually went off in search of game for the supper pot, or to acquire supplies of duck, goose, or deer for consumption the following day. If game was scarce, no northman refused a meal of fish, particularly the rich, firm flesh of the whitefish or its near relative, the *inconnu*, which were easily netted in large quantities and quickly broiled over the camp fire. Unlike a number of other bourgeois, Mackenzie did not abuse his men or take them for granted. He worked them hard, but made every effort to ensure that they were well-fed. It was common practice for him to give them a tot of rum after a particularly trying day. And it is clear that he tried on this voyage (without much success) to share with them some of the wonder of discovery—in seeing for the first time the strange flora and fauna beyond the Arctic Circle, and the phenomenon of the midnight sun.

Promptly at four on the morning of June 4, the party was on its way down the Rivière des Rochers, one of a number of channels through which some of the mighty spring overflow of the Peace River rushes south into Lake Athabasca. Thirty miles later they were on the broad, silt-laden waters of the Slave River, which is the name the Peace assumes on its northward journey after it absorbs the Rochers. Ahead of them on the Slave were several portages, the only ones they had to make all the way to the Arctic. At one, an Indian's canoe drifted loose and was smashed to pieces as it went down a set of rapids.

For the next few days the weather was rainy and chilly. On the sixth there was a sudden cold spell and "the Indians made use of their mittens." Two days later the rain was so heavy and a north wind so violent that Mackenzie was forced to remain encamped beside the river. At two-thirty the next morning, a foggy but calm one, he roused his men and set off downstream again. By nine o'clock they had reached Great Slave Lake, where everyone suddenly felt a biting chill in the air. The huge lake was entirely covered with ice, which was unbroken except close to the shore.

Held up for several days until drenching rainstorms and blustery winds had broken up the ice, Mackenzie had plenty of time to observe his surroundings. He quickly noted the considerable permafrost condition: the ground, a mixture of clay and sand, had thawed out to a depth of only eighteen inches and thus prevented any noticeable growth of plant life except trees. However, the region was rich in wildlife.

> The beavers, which are numerous, build their houses in small lakes and rivers, which they cannot do in the large river [the Slave] as the ice carries everything along with it in the spring. All the banks of the river [the Slave] are covered with wild fowl. We killed two swans, ten geese, and one beaver this morning without losing an hour's time; so that if we were out for the purpose of hunting we might soon fill our canoe. . . . Fish for our supper [was] inconnu, whitefish, trout, carp &c. Two of our hunters killed a reindeer [caribou] and a young one. . . .

The wildlife also included a large insect population. Mackenzie remarks wryly in his journal entry for the twelfth that, upon the weather becoming clear with westerly winds, his party encountered "old companions", mosquitoes who "visit us in greater numbers than we would wish as they are very troublesome guests."

Always aware of the need to conserve his pemmican supplies, Mackenzie encouraged the women in the party to gather berries of various sorts and personally accompanied one of his men to a nearby island, where the two picked up dozens of swan, geese, and duck eggs. He was wise to take food where he found it because for the next few days fishing yielded nothing but a few pike, and then for a time ice floes were carried inshore and denied his men the use of the fishing nets. An added drain on his supplies occurred with the arrival of three Indian families, who had to be fed if their good will was to be retained.

Dodging hurriedly from island to island, it took the party a whole week to cross a thirty-five-mile stretch of Great Slave Lake to its north shore. Despite high winds and torrential rainstorms, the men managed to prevent their frail canoes from being crushed by rampaging ice floes or ripped open by sheet ice. Mackenzie remarks upon the speed with which the latter formed, even late in the month of June. He sat up all night on the twenty-first to observe the setting and rising of the sun, an interval of only four hours and twenty-two minutes at that latitude. During this time—the shortest period of darkness all summer at that latitude— the lake's surface froze so hard that it "crusted" with ice an eighth of an inch thick.

On June 23 Mackenzie landed on the barren, rocky north shore and met three lodges of Yellowknife Indians, one of whom was sent off to fetch the members of other lodges living close by. These natives offered him beaver and marten skins but could not give him what he really wanted—positive information about the river that emptied out of the lake's western end, although one Indian thought that he had seen the beginnings of such a waterway. (He was immediately engaged as the party's guide.) Ever the business-minded Scot, Mackenzie lectured the Yellowknives sternly on the benefits they would derive from trapping and promised them a trading post, which would be maintained "as long as they would deserve it."

On the twenty-fifth, leaving Leroux behind to pass the summer trading along the north shore, Mackenzie and his party paddled west in search of the waterway that Pond had said drained out of Great Slave Lake. They moved rapidly from point to point across the many bays that indented the north shore, keeping a nervous lookout for partly submerged ice sheets and for sudden changes of wind and sky that warned of squalls or storms. Despite the long, tiring hours spent each day on the water, there was little rest for the party at night. Whether they encamped on land or on an offshore island, swarms of mosquitoes and flies attacked them with exhausting persistence. The journal entry for the twenty-seventh begins by suggesting that everyone was glad to start canoeing at three o'clock in the morning after "a very restless night being tormented by mosquitoes."

It was on the twenty-seventh that their guide directed them into a deep bay, which he thought might be the entrance to the river. But its waters lacked any clear sign of a current and brought them up against masses of broken ice, whose presence was made even more menacing by slowly drifting patches of fog. Backpaddling very carefully, the explorers finally found refuge for the night on a nearby island. The same disappointment was suffered again the following day after they coursed down a long bay that led westward. This time the guide assured them that they would arrive at the river. But, after hours of paddling, the canoes scraped to a halt in shallow waters. English Chief, in a passion of rage, promptly threatened to shoot the Yellowknife. Mackenzie doesn't say whether or not fear improved a lazy memory, but at this point the guide suddenly recalled journeying from the river through wooded country to the very spot where the canoes were now beached.

The guide was right—or a lucky guesser. The party broke camp at four the next morning, backtracked out of the bay, rounded yet another headland, and soon detected a strong, smooth current taking them out of Great Slave Lake. Later that day, a stiff breeze from the eastward drove the party downriver under sail at a very brisk rate. Mackenzie must have been elated: having fixed Great Slave as being at 61° 40′N—approximately the latitude of "Cook's River"—he was now on a major waterway leading westward.

On July 3 he calculated that they had run downstream 217 miles west and 44 miles north. (Mackenzie continually underestimated the force of the current: the party averaged one hundred miles a day going downstream.) Sooner or later he expected the river to pierce the Rockies and lead to the Pacific. The current, which "makes such a hissing . . . as a kettle moderately boiling," quickened to eight or ten knots in some stretches. He recorded that his Indians "complain much of our hard marching, that they are not accustomed to such hard fatigue." Mackenzie completely ignored their plaint.

There is only one note of disappointment in his

Preceding page:

A composite of thirteen photographs, this illustration epitomizes the stark landscape of the Canadian North, which is here silhouetted by the phenomenon of the "midnight sun." The waters are those of Great Bear Lake, N. W. T., 12,000 square miles in extent and the largest freshwater lake located wholly within Canada. It drains into the Mackenzie River via Great Bear River.

Late on the evening of July 10, 1789, Mackenzie made camp about four hundred miles downstream from the mouth of Great Bear River. (By his own reckoning he was at 67° 47'N and was therefore within the Arctic Circle). He writes in the Voyages *that he sat up all that night "to observe at what time the sun would set, but found that it did not set at all." This is rather a puzzling statement because Mackenzie could not possibly have experienced an entire 24 hours of daylight in the month of July, even at this northern latitude. In latitudes north of 66° after June 21, darkness creeps back again until it becomes a daily phenomenon.*

National Film Board. Information Canada Photothèque.

journal at this time: when the weather warmed up from time to time, he was defeated by his "old companions." One day he halted to climb to the top of a prominent "hill" and view the surrounding land. Accompanied by two Canadians and the Chipewyans, it took an hour and a quarter to ascend what proved to be a small mountain. They had barely time to get their breath back and look around when "we were obliged to shorten our stay here on account of the swarms of mosquitoes that attacked us and were the only inhabitants of the place." On another occasion, when he and a Chipewyan again attempted to climb a high hill, "We were obliged to relinquish our design halfway up it, being nearly suffocated by swarms of mosquitoes."

However, as day succeeded day, the river flowed steadily northwest, and the mountains always remained tantalizingly at a distance to the west. Early on the morning of July 5 in the neighbourhood of modern Fort Norman, Mackenzie received a faint hint about where he was heading. He went ashore to speak with a small group of Slaves and Dogribs, all of whom were "an ugly, meagre, ill-made people" and many of whom "appeared sickly, owing as I imagine to their dirty way of living." Their vague information about the river "had so much of the fabulous" about it, including "many monsters (which can only exist in their imaginations)," that he ignored the kernel of truth in their statement that the explorers "would be several winters getting to the sea and that we should be old men by the time we would return." English Chief and his men were much depressed by this information because they were already tired of the voyage and also feared that the farther north the party advanced the scarcer game would become. But Mackenzie persuaded them otherwise and even induced them to bribe a Dogrib with presents of kettles, an axe, and a knife to join the party.

Pushing on down the island-studded river the explorers soon came to where it had gouged out of the landscape a trench so deep that sheer limestone walls towered two hundred feet above the water for a distance of seven miles—the famous Ramparts of the Mackenzie River, just south of modern Norman Wells. Farther downstream the land on either side began to flatten out noticeably, and the river banks were low and slimy with mud. Moving through this region, which he called "Eskmeaux" territory, Mackenzie only came across Eskimo litter in deserted summer campsites. Outside huts lay whale-bone canoe and sledge frames and round pieces of poplar bark used as corks to buoy up fishing nets made of animal sinews. Inside were

> . . . a square stone kettle, [which] could contain about 2 gallons; it's very surprising how they could have dug it out. The bottom is flat . . . several wooden dishes and troughs . . . many bones of large-size fish and part of two big heads, we don't know of what animal. I suppose the Sea Horses!

By the tenth, his observations told him he was at "67.47 North latitude, which is farther north than I had expected." According to the sun and his sextant, he was nowhere near Cook's River and was clearly not on one of its tributaries. And a Hare guide he had picked up along the way to replace the obviously desertion-minded Dogrib knew of no river other than the one on which they were travelling. According to his information, Mackenzie would come in ten days to the sea and three days later meet with Eskimos who had formerly made war upon the Hares. The guide knew nothing about the sea but a little about the Eskimos: they lived around the sea and had "very large canoes in which 4 or 5 families embark," killed a large fish—which Mackenzie presumed to be a whale—a great number of white bears, and "another large animal, but our hunters could not understand the description he gave of it." (The fish was probably a seal; the bears would be polar bears; the other animal may have been a muskox.) Even the landscape suggested a huge delta because they had now come to a region where the river widened enormously and filtered its way through channels banked with mud and sand, which were so various that "we were at a loss what channel out of some hundred to take."

Passing through mile after mile of country where only four inches of topsoil had thawed out and thus "scarce a shrub was to be seen," Mackenzie and his men were approaching the Arctic Ocean. He tacitly admits this in the journal entry for July

12, when he calculated his latitude as 69°N, because he speaks of landing that day "at the boundary of our voyage in this direction." Together with English Chief—who had remained with the party only because Mackenzie had "presented" him with one of his own travelling coats—he stood on the highest part of an island and viewed solid ice as far as the eye could see "from the south-west by compass to the eastward." He had come to the Hyperborean Sea, as he often termed Arctic waters. Mackenzie voices his deep disappointment indirectly by referring to his voyageurs, who

> . . .express much sorrow that they are obliged to return without seeing the [Western] sea, in which I believe them sincere for we marched exceeding hard coming down the river, and I never heard them grumble; but on the contrary in good spirits and in hopes every day that the next would bring them to the Mer d'Ouest [Western Sea], and declare themselves now ready to go with me wherever I choose to lead them.

Yet, with the dogged persistence so characteristic of him, Mackenzie at first refused to accept that he had arrived at Pond's "Ice Sea." This is clear from two incidents on the twelfth and thirteenth when encamped on what he ultimately named Whale Island (probably the modern Garry Island) at 69°14′ North. On the night of the twelfth, the party had no sooner gone to bed than some of the men had to get up and move the baggage "on account of the water rising." Mackenzie ascribed the phenomenon to a high wind. The next morning he either ignored or preferred not to comment on yet another indication of the presence nearby of salt water: the nets held several fish, one of which, about the size of a herring, "none of us know, except the English Chief, who says they are very plentiful at Hudson's Bay." On the morning of the fourteenth Mackenzie even encouraged his men to chase what he recognized as white whales, although he does not remark upon the obvious conclusion. But he knew that he could go no farther.

> This morning I fixed a post close by our campment, on which I engraved the latitude of the place, my own name,

Preceding page:

This watery maze of lake, pond, slough, and swamp is a typical scene in the Mackenzie Delta. A little over twice the size of Prince Edward Island, the Delta is a mighty labyrinth of hundreds of miles of winding river channels and thousands of lakes both large and small. Like the Athabasca country, the Delta is four-fifths drowned and when not frozen is half-hidden by mosquitoes and black flies.

Canadian Government Travel Bureau Photograph.

and the number of men with me, and the time we had been here.

Mackenzie spent two more days in the river delta dodging fogbanks and ice floes while trying to establish the extent of the vast semicircular bay to which he had come. On the fifteenth, the water again rose during the early hours and soaked the baggage, and this time he was forced to admit that "as the wind had not changed nor blew harder than when we went to bed, we were all of the opinion that it was the tide." He tried to confirm that the water was tidal, but a storm blew up and made this impossible. On the chilly, rainy morning of the sixteenth, he calculated roughly that there was a rise of water level as much as sixteen or eighteen inches and was at last convinced that he was at the northern sea or on one of its coastal lagoons.

Mackenzie knew, too, from his soundings of the "lake," as he called the delta, that it was too shallow to the westward to permit even a canoe to float. In some places between the icefields and the shore there was barely a foot of water. The short northern summer was almost over, and he was unable to advance northward or westward. In addition, his supply of provisions was running dangerously low and he had thirteen hungry followers to feed. This was a major problem. As he ruefully remarks, "I always found northmen blessed with good appetites, but nothing equal to what ours are and have been since we entered this river. I would have thought it gluttinous in my men, did I not find that my own appetite has augmented in proportion to theirs." There was nothing to do but backtrack as quickly as possible before winter imprisoned them all somewhere along the hundreds of miles between Whale Island and Fort Chipewyan.

Short of food and time, Mackenzie pushed his men hard, and the return journey severely tested their stamina. For much of it they were forced to "track" or haul the canoes by means of shoulder harnesses attached to bow and stern, which meant either ploughing through river debris in the sometimes muddy, sometimes sandy shallows or stumbling painfully over stones and boulders as they waded breast-high through icy water. The weather still varied wildly from oppressively hot days to ones on which bitingly cold winds swept down from the Arctic "and we can't put clothes enough on to keep us warm." On two occasions storms blew down their tents, and during one of these the wind was so violent that "we were obliged to throw ourselves flat on the ground to escape being wounded by the stones that were hurled about by the air like sand." As on the downward trip, the party was once again subjected to "the persecution of the mosquitoes." Yet the men averaged 30 miles a day going upstream, and the party was back at Fort Chipewyan in just under two months, having completed in 102 days a round trip of almost 3000 miles, the equivalent of a direct coast-to-coast journey between Halifax, Nova Scotia, and Vancouver, British Columbia. The river section of the voyage was itself a fantastic performance on the part of the northmen, who had made the downward run in 14 days but only took 38 days to fight their way back against the unrelenting current. Several modern canoeists who have travelled the Mackenzie both ways with lighter loads confess their inability to come anywhere near matching this record.

Mackenzie does not record his private thoughts as his men laboured upstream on what he is said to have called the "River Disappointment." But he was still determined to find a way to "Cook's River." As a matter of fact, his stubborn refusal to accept defeat in anything he attempted to do was so great that at one point in the return journey it nearly cost him his life.

On August 10, by which time the explorers were about 100 miles south of the Liard River, the mountains west of the river seemed to be as close as they had at any point in the entire journey. At least they did to an impatient, curious Mackenzie, and he decided to climb one of them to see the nature of the land to the westward. He landed and, together with an Indian companion, walked briskly away from the river. After an hour spent plunging through thick underbrush and a further two hours dodging through stands of white birch, poplar, and pines, his objective

. . . appeared as far from us as when we had seen them from the river. My companion wanted absolutely to return;

his shoes and leggings were all torn to pieces. . . . However I persisted in proceeding and that we would pass the night in the mountains and return in the morning. As we approached them, the ground became quite marshy, and we waded in water and grass up to the middle [of our bodies], till we came within a mile of the foot of the mountains, when I fell in up to the arm-pits, and with some difficulty I extricated myself. I found it impossible to proceed in a straight line; and the marsh extended as far as I could see so that I did not attempt to make the circuit [of it]: so therefore thought it most prudent to make the best of my way back to my canoe (tho' it was night), when I arrived after 12 o'clock, very much fatigued.

The episode is an excellent example of Mackenzie's ability to push himself (and others) to the limits of physical and mental endurance, but not pig-headedly beyond the limits of common sense.

It was in the course of the return journey that Mackenzie first heard native echoes of Europeans on the Pacific. The first occasion was when a band of Indians recounted an Eskimo report of meeting white men "in large canoes" far to the westward "eight or ten winters since" and exchanging leather for iron. (This contact might have been with Captain Cook but was more likely with Russian traders somewhere on the northwest coast of Alaska.) Some days later he talked with a Dogrib, who repeated a Hare Indian story of a mighty river on the other side of the western mountains that fell into the "White Man's Lake" far to the northwest. (At this point Mackenzie was so far north that these references were probably to the Yukon River and the North Pacific Ocean.) The Dogrib said that the natives who lived at the river mouth made "canoes larger than ours," which tallied with Cook's descriptions of Pacific coast dugouts and war canoes, and killed "a kind of large beaver, the skin of which is almost red," which was unmistakably a description of the sea otter. Using beads as a bribe, Mackenzie induced another native to trace a sand map of the river for him. This time, Mackenzie picked up the information that there was a trading post at its mouth, which "I took to be Unalaska Fort, and consequently the river to the west to be Cook's river." (This was optimistic but mistaken guesswork. The mouth of the Yukon is on the west coast of Alaska. "Cook's River" was reported to be on the south coast.)

The only reason Mackenzie didn't clamber up and over the mountains right there and then was that the Indian refused the explorer's attempts to hire him as a guide. In fact, Mackenzie was puzzled and annoyed to find that all his Indian informants became strangely lacking in confidence—or suddenly became ill—when he suggested that they lead him over the mountains. Since his Chipewyan interpreters had often indicated their weariness with the voyage, he strongly suspected that they were misrepresenting what they were told in order to avoid further exploration. Finally, towards the end of the journey upstream, Mackenzie lost his temper with the Chipewyans.

The cause of the incident was an order to English Chief and his followers to contact a number of Indians Mackenzie had spotted on the river bank and engage them in friendly conversation. As usual, he intended to join in after a while and make enquiries about the country on the west side of the mountains. However, the Indians ran off. The Chipewyans made no attempt to follow them and casually began to pick at the few possessions the natives had left behind in their panicky flight. This was too much for Mackenzie.

I severely rebuked the English Chief. I ordered him, his young men, and my own men to go and look out for the Indians. I went also, but they were much too frightened and had too much the start of us to overtake them. English Chief was very much displeased that I had reproached him, and told me so. I had waited for such an opportunity to tell him [what I thought of] his behaviour to me for some time past, told him that I had more reason to be angry than he, that I had come a great way at great expense to no purpose, and that I thought he hid from me a part of what the natives told him respecting the country, for fear he should have to follow me. . . .

Mackenzie's explosion of anger was undoubtedly the

result of pent-up frustration. He had exposed himself and his voyageurs to great danger. He had endured the nagging fear of hunger as he had led them twice through bleak, barren regions that sometimes failed to provide adequate supplies of game or fish. He had been very patient when local Indians failed to provide him with reliable advice and guidance on the northward leg of the voyage. Now, as he was still trying to justify the voyage, his own Indians were again foiling attempts to find "Cook's River."

After a couple of hours, Mackenzie calmed down. He placated English Chief that evening by inviting him to supper, which was preceded by a dram or two of rum, and took care to send him back to his tent later with "a little grog to drown his chagrin." All apart from his need of the Chief and his followers to hunt and interpret, Mackenzie must have realized that the Chipewyan's instinct was sound: it was far too late in the season to go chasing off over mountains on a vaguely promising trail. He was simply going to have to accept the bitter fact that he had not found a way to the Pacific. The expedition had been a total failure—or so he thought. But then Mackenzie had no way of knowing that he had explored and charted the North American river that is exceeded in length only by the mighty Mississippi river system.

The Second Exploration, 1793

*I*n 1790 Mackenzie remarked in a letter to Roderic that at the July meeting of the partners at Grand Portage, "My Expedition is hardly spoken of but this is what I expected." It had been unsuccessful. It had not led to the Pacific and had not brought in new profits. A party of French Canadians and Indians had been paid and fed for almost three and a half months at Company expense, yet the gross profit was the packs of beaver and marten skins that Leroux had been able to purchase on the north shore of Great Slave Lake, pelts that he might well have secured on his own that summer.

The exploration, however, did have important results. It proved that there was no practicable route to the Pacific in high latitudes. Even at the height of the northern summer, there was no way westward through the Arctic ice. Secondly, Mackenzie had demolished a great historic myth by demonstrating that there was no northwest passage through the continent. Thirdly, he had discovered that the "River Disappointment" itself ran through several thousand square miles of fur-rich territory. (In fact the entire Mackenzie drainage basin is close to 700,000 square miles in extent—a region almost twice the size of Ontario or British Columbia.) Lastly, the basic reason for his journey held good because a way to the Pacific still had to be found.

No details of the reactions of Mackenzie's fellow-partners to his explorations have come down to us. Presumably they listened politely to the account he gave of it. It could only have been a polite interest because there is no evidence that they or the Montreal agents used this new geographic knowledge, as they had used Pond's speculations, to influence British authorities in Quebec and London into giving the Company a trading monopoly in the Northwest. However Mackenzie's colleagues probably were keenly attentive when he estimated the potential trade of the region north of Great Slave Lake.

Eight days after Mackenzie told Roderic of the lack of interest in his expedition, a new Company share agreement was signed, under whose terms the explorer would receive two of twenty shares, double his previous holding. His voyage had been something of a failure, but management still rated him highly.

Long after his return to Athabasca, Mackenzie decided that the Pacific could be reached by the "Great River which falls into the Sea to the Westward of the river in which I voyaged." The only trouble was that the more he questioned Indians, the more he seemed to hear of *two* great rivers beyond the Rocky Mountains: they were variously described as the "Great River of the West" and the "river that runs towards the midday sun." (Mackenzie must have been getting bits and pieces of information about what we now call the Columbia and the Fraser. At this time, no one suspected that there might be two great river systems west of the mountains.) Evidently both waterways led to the 'White Man's Lake," but did so far to the south. Yet the reports were so often confusing that Mackenzie decided he was really hearing about one large waterway. In any case, there was no denying the large flow of fresh water at the end of Cook Inlet, and there were strong reports of a river running northwest in the general direction of the Inlet (which is what the Yukon does for a time). Logically, he stood a better chance of reaching the west coast by seeking "Cook's River," initially by going up the Peace River, which Pond had said led through the barrier of the Rocky Mountains.

Late in 1792, Mackenzie prepared for his second attempt to find a water route to and from the Pacific. As before, the faithful Roderic would stand in for him at Fort Chipewyan.

The second, and by far the largest, travel section of the *Voyages from Montreal* is entitled "Journal of A Second Voyage &c." and begins:

October 10, 1792. Having made every necessary preparation, I left Fort Chipewyan to proceed up the Peace River. I had resolved to go as far as our most distant settlement, which would occupy the remaining part of the season. . . . I proposed to attempt my next discovery across the mountains from the source of that river.

If he was going to get to the Pacific and back in the course of a summer season, the nearer the ocean he started, the better. After wintering as far up the Peace as possible, he would be able to make a quick dash westward and hurry back to Fort Chipewyan before winter closed in again.

Early that October morning, Mackenzie's tiny brigade of three canoes paddled across the choppy, green waters of Lake Athabasca. Two days later they turned westward into the mile-wide, muddy mouth of the Peace River.* As on the trip to the Arctic, the canoes had been equipped by Mackenzie with masts and sails, which, when the winds were northeasterly, helped the party to make good headway. They had to hurry along. The weather was bitterly cold, and ice formed on the river every night.

At 8 A.M. on the nineteenth, the party came to an abandoned Company post and found it wreathed in smoke and flames. They all hurried ashore and were able to save some of the smaller huts, cursing the men who had stopped off there overnight and had carelessly left a fire burning in the main building. Later that day Mackenzie caught up with the miscreants, a canoe party led by John Finlay,** a Company clerk and a son of Mackenzie's old employer, who was on his way to winter at another Peace River post. At six o'clock the next morning the two groups arrived together at Finlay's destination

> ... amid the rejoicing and firing [of guns] of the people, who were animated with the prospect of again indulging themselves in the luxury of rum, of which they have been deprived since the beginning of May, as it is a practice throughout the Northwest neither to sell or give any rum to the natives during the summer. . . .

*Mackenzie remarks that the waterway derives its name from Peace Point, a natural feature about 20 miles from the mouth of the river and "the spot where the Knisteneaux [Cree] and Beaver Indians settled their dispute." Here Cree invaders from the valley of the Churchill, who had driven what they called the "Slave" Indians into northern Athabasca and the Beavers into western Athabasca, agreed upon a common boundary with the latter.

**Five years later Finlay ascended the Peace and explored its northern branch, which has since borne his name.

There were frequent changes of the weather in the course of the day, and it froze rather hard in the night. The thickness of the ice in the morning was a sufficient notice for me to proceed.

Mackenzie left the next morning. For several days he drove his voyageurs hard and on the first of November managed to reach the place that had been chosen as his wintering quarters, a site five or six miles west along the Peace from its junction with the Smoky (the site of modern Peace River, Alberta). Awaiting him were two men who had been sent ahead in the spring to square timbers and cut palisades. A large number of Indians had gathered to welcome him with volleys of musket shot. Mackenzie called them to him and gave each about four inches of tobacco and a dram of spirits. Then he told them he had heard that they had been very troublesome to his predecessor (Peter Pond) and that he had come to find out if this was so, adding that he would treat them kindly—if they deserved it. Mackenzie made it quite clear that he would also be hard on them if they failed to bring the returns in furs that he expected from them. To this end, he spent the next six days equipping the Indians for their winter hunting and also arranging for the provisioning of his post with fresh meat. Only when this was done did Mackenzie give his full attention to the construction of Fort Fork.

By now the river was becoming choked with ice, which put an end to all navigation. Day after day ice jams piled up. By the twenty-second the swift-flowing Peace was frozen over. It was to be the end of April before he and his men saw running water again and "were visited by our summer companions, the gnats and mosquitoes."

Unfortunately for the voyageurs the first bitter breaths of winter made the labour of construction difficult and very tiring. On November 27, with the temperature hovering around the zero mark for the fourth successive day, little or no work could be done: the effect of the frost was such that the axes became as brittle as glass. It was almost Christmas before Mackenzie was able to move out of his tent and into the house erected for him, while the men hurried to construct bunkhouses for themselves and storehouses for the winter's take in pelts. At this point in his journal, Mackenzie displays great compassion for those he calls "my people":

> . . . it is necessary to describe in some measure the hardships which they undergo without a murmur, in order to convey a general notion of them.

> The men who were now with me left this place [Athabasca] in the beginning of last May and went to the Rainy Lake [the depot for the Athabasca brigades 1500 miles to the east] in canoes laden with packs of furs which, from the immense length of the voyage and other concurring circumstances, is a most severe trial of patience and perseverance. There they did not remain a sufficient time for ordinary repose because they take a load of goods in exchange and proceed on their return, in a great measure, day and night. They have been back almost two months and all that time have been continually engaged in very toilsome labour, with nothing more than a common shed to protect them from the frost and snow. Such is the life which these people lead and is continued with unremitting exertion, till their strength is lost in premature old age.

On the first day of January 1793, Mackenzie was awakened at daybreak by musket shots. In a company largely run by Highland Scots, Christmas was more or less another working day, but the wintering partners had encouraged their canoemen to celebrate New Year's Day with gusto. Mackenzie took the hint and hastened to give them plenty of spirits and a special issue of flour with which to make cakes. The new year was only a few days old when two "Rocky Mountain Indians" (Beaver Indians) turned up at Fort Fork with the information that just beyond the mountains was a great waterway running towards the midday sun. They also informed Mackenzie that all the way to the mountains the countryside of the Peace was abundant with animals. This seemed a good omen of success. It was also a great relief. Like every trader, Mackenzie's perpetual problem was finding enough game and fish to be able to conserve pemmican

The Second Exploration, 1793

supplies against those unpredictable times when game became scarce or disappeared completely.

But two events a few months later bitterly disappointed him. The Indians of the region proved to be poor hunters. Early in May he had only six canoe loads of furs to send back to Fort Chipewyan. Secondly, he had had great trouble securing Indian guides. At one point he managed to engage three, but one, who claimed to have been on a very large river two days' march west of the mountains, deserted him the day before Mackenzie set off to go through the mountains, and "the two remaining lads knew no more of the country than I do myself."

Mackenzie was also greatly troubled by doubts of the wisdom of what he was attempting. In a letter to Roderic penned the night before he set off west, he wrote first that matters were "too far advanced [on the undertaking] not to make some attempt." Farther on in the same letter, he confessed:

> I never was so undecided in my intentions as this year regarding my going to the [Grand] Portage or remaining inland. I weighed everything in my mind over and over again. . . . I begin to think it is the height of folly in a man to reside in a country of this kind, deprived of every comfort that can render life agreeable, especially when he has a competency to enjoy life in civilized society. . . .
>
> I hardly know what [I] am about therefore will conclude here 'till tomorrow. . . .
> Adieu, Dear Roderic
> Yours unchangeably

The loneliness of command, which his own reserved manner did nothing to improve, and the isolation of a frontier post in winter were beginning to affect his nerves and his judgment. In addition, he was probably suffering from fear and apprehension at the thought of again taking off into the unknown. But of course he would go on, driven by his determination to succeed whatever the cost.

On the evening of May 9, Mackenzie set off west up

the Peace River. He took with him as his second-in-command, Alexander McKay, a Company clerk, six voyageurs (two of whom, Joseph Landry and Charles Ducette, had accompanied him to the Arctic), and two Indian guides. They all travelled in a canoe built to Mackenzie's specifications. It was large enough to carry the ten men (and a dog) and three thousand pounds of provisions, goods, ammunition, and baggage, yet on a good portage two men could carry it for three miles without resting.

For the next few days the countryside was very beautiful, gently rising back from a river front edged with alder and willow, grassy and almost lawn-like in places, and dotted with groves of poplar. As the two Beaver Indians had said, it was rich in animal life, particularly buffalo and elk, which were present in vast herds. And Mackenzie was relieved to see plenty of white (paper) birch, the bark of which could be employed in canoe repairs. The only adverse entry in his journal at this point, apart from noting wet, windy weather accompanied by occasional freezing temperatures overnight, mentions the sighting of "two grisly and hideous bears." In the early afternoon of the seventeenth, at which point they were just a little west of present-day Fort St. John, British Columbia, all of them were cheered to see the Rocky Mountains appear to the westward, their summits shrouded in snow. Things were going well. Paddling or poling, the men were making between ten and twenty miles a day against the spring-swollen waters of the Peace.

Two days later they approached a section of the river that Indians had warned Mackenzie was a succession of rapids, cascades, and falls, which were always bypassed in the course of a day's march. This was a portage north of the Peace River Canyon. Had he taken it from the start Mackenzie would have avoided a great deal of toil and trouble. But he didn't realize what he was letting himself in for and directed his men up the south side of the canyon.

After towing the heavily loaded canoe for about a mile, the party was forced by overhanging rock to cross over to the north side, where stones loosened by spring thaws and recent rains were continually slipping or rolling down into the river. The bank itself was steep, and the men were having trouble enough finding their footing without being knocked off balance by falling debris or having stones slide out from under their moccasined feet. Mackenzie climbed to the top of the bank to view the route ahead and call out warnings and instructions down to his men— uselessly, as it turned out, because the steady roar of the tumbling waters completely drowned out his shouts.

> And here I could not but reflect with infinite anxiety on the hazard of my enterprise. One false step of those who were attached to the line, or the breaking of the line itself, would have at once consigned the canoe and everything it contained to instant destruction.

In the course of the next two miles, the rapids were so bad that the party—including Mackenzie—had to portage the canoe's contents no less than five times.

For three exhausting days they fought the Peace River, until "it began to be muttered on all sides that there was no alternative but to return." Yet for all their labours, when Mackenzie climbed part way up the side of the canyon he could see nothing but a steady succession of rapids and falls within an ever-widening canyon. Since the river route was impassable, at daybreak on the twenty-second Mackenzie struck off across country over what turned out to be a seven-mile mountain trail. In so doing he avoided the horror of twenty-five miles of tumbling, seething waters, in the course of which the Peace drops almost 250 feet and races wildly through a narrow gorge whose walls are often sheer for a thousand feet or more.

And so they began what even the habitually imperturbable Mackenzie admits was an "an extraordinary journey."

> The men began without delay to cut a road up the mountain, and as the trees were but of small growth, I ordered them to fell these which they found convenient in such a manner that they might fall parallel with the road [being made], but at the same time not separate them entirely from the stumps, so that they might form a kind of railing on either side . . . the whole party proceeded with no small

degree of apprehension to fetch the canoe . . . we advanced with it up the mountain, having the lines [of rope] doubled and fastened successively as we went on to the stumps; while a man at the end of it hauled it round a tree, holding it on and shifting it as we proceeded; so that we may be said, with strict truth, to have warped the canoe up the mountain.

It was two o'clock in the afternoon before the canoe and all its baggage had been hauled up to the top. Mackenzie allowed his men to rest for three hours and then ordered them to cut a road through the light timber and thick underbrush that stretched ahead for several miles. At four o'clock the next morning they were portaging the canoe's contents while he himself, McKay, and the two Indian guides hacked away with the axes. By five in the afternoon the canoe and its load had been advanced a further three miles, although everyone was in "a state of fatigue that may be more readily conceived than expressed." The next day was spent in similar fashion, this time in cutting their way up and down several hills. Mercifully they came to the river again before nightfall. In the course of the portage their clothes had been ripped and shredded by the prickles of the tall devil's club plant or torn by numerous briar, gooseberry, and currant bushes along the trail; their bodies ached from their exertions; and their senses were dulled from lack of sleep and sheer tiredness. But at least they were alive. Mackenzie and his men would never have survived the maelstrom of mad waters in the horseshoe-shaped canyon of the Peace.

At the western end of the portage, the men spent half a day trimming stout tree branches with which to pole the canoe upriver and ease to some extent the hard labour of paddling against the powerful current. And here the business-like Mackenzie left a visiting card for local Indians, as a friendly gesture and as an invitation to trade: he erected a pole, and attached to it a packet containing a knife, a steel flint, beads, and a few other minor articles.

As they journeyed westward some days later, snow-capped peaks towered on either side of them—the Rocky Mountains. It was almost the end of May and the sun shone clearly, but the dry cold of the region was so penetrating that even the hardy voyageurs complained of its numbing effect on their hands as they worked the poles. The weather was so bitter that the men had to wear their blanket coats day and night. To keep them good humoured, Mackenzie gave them an issue of rum (a *régale*), usually at the end of each day's labour. By May 29 a whole keg had been consumed. Indeed, the weather was so cold on the thirty-first that he called a halt at nine in the morning with the intention of kindling a fire to thaw out his half-frozen men— "a very uncommon circumstance at this season." However, a quicker solution was found: "a small quantity of rum served as an adequate substitute."

Although he does not say so at this particular point in the *Voyages*, Mackenzie had to keep his men going by an admixture of his own cool, calm behaviour and generous hand-outs of liquor. May 19, the day they entered the lower Peace Canyon, must have been an experience that shattered the men's confidence in themselves. Hitherto they had mastered all the waters of the Northwest. Until that day, they had never encountered the fury and menace of a mountain river in flood, particularly one which, even in Mackenzie's matter-of-fact prose, was "one white sheet of foaming water." The Peace at this point was—and still is—unnavigable in a birchbark canoe. After the traverse around the Canyon, Mackenzie kept his terrified, near-mutinous men moving westward for weeks on his own reserves of will power and courage. The only thing he feared was failure to complete his task of discovery.

By May 31 they had passed through the Rocky Mountains and come to what in later years was called Finlay Forks,* where the Finlay River, racing down the Rocky Mountain Trench from the northwest, joined the Parsnip River from the southeast to form the Peace River. West of the Forks was a chain of mountains "running south and north as far as the eye could reach." Which waterway were they to take?

---

*Now submerged beneath the storage lake forming behind the W. A. C. Bennett Dam. This massive structure, 600 feet high and 7000 feet long, straddles the Peace River almost on top of the spot where Mackenzie completed his portage around the Peace Canyon.

Preceding page:
This scene illustrates the basic difficulty Mackenzie faced on his voyage to the Pacific. He was seeking a direct route west, yet even after passing through the Rocky Mountains his way was barred by range after range of mountains running north and south.

Mackenzie was lucky at the start. While there are many passes within or across the Rocky Mountains, there are only four natural breaches in the 1000-mile length in Canada of this massive wall of stone and ice. One of these is the Peace River, the only waterway to pierce the entire mountain chain between the Yukon and New Mexico. The Peace led him to the Parsnip River in that extraordinary feature we call the Rocky Mountain Trench, a long trough anywhere from two to ten miles wide that separates the Canadian Rockies from the other western ranges. Thereafter he had to find a way between or around mountain chains, over the plateau country of the British Columbia interior, and then through the towering coastal ranges.

The Finlay led north and looked easier, and the men made it plain that it was their choice. Mackenzie agreed "as it appeared to me to be the most likely to bring us nearest to the part where I wished to fall on the Pacific Ocean." But he recalled that an aged Beaver warrior he had met earlier that year at Fort Fork had advised him

> ... not on any account to follow it [the Finlay], as it was soon lost in various branches among the mountains, and that there was no great river that ran in any direction near it; but by following the latter [the Parsnip], we should arrive at a carrying-place to another large river, that did not exceed a day's march, where the inhabitants build houses and live upon islands. . . . There was so much apparent truth in the old man's narrative that I determined to be governed by it.

He ordered the steersmen to proceed up the swifter, narrower Parsnip, and it was a crucial decision. The Finlay would have led the party to where the headwaters of the Liard, Skeena, and Stikine rivers interlock in a maze of streams; in all likelihood they would have lost their way completely. Very sensibly, Mackenzie heeded the old man's warning, although as a result he had to endure days of bitter complaint from his men and, worse still, occasional doubts as to the wisdom of his choice.

The canoe had hardly been a few hours on the Parsnip when Mackenzie had to use both sympathy and sternness to keep his men going.

> ... the rush of water was so powerful that we were the greatest part of the afternoon in getting two or three miles—a very tardy and mortifying progress, and which, with the voyage, was openly execrated by many of those who were engaged in it; and the inexpressible toil these people had endured, as well as the dangers they had encountered, required some degree of consideration. I therefore employed those arguments which were best calculated to calm their immediate discontents, as well as to encourage their future hopes; though at the same time I delivered my sentiments in

such a manner as to convince them that I was determined to proceed.

But he was greatly encouraged by clear evidence of beaver colonies. "In no part of the North-West did I see so much beaver-work . . . as in the course of this day. In some places they had cut down several acres of large poplars, and we also saw a great number of these active and sagacious animals."

Paddling occasionally, but more often poling against the strong current, the canoemen moved their craft over the wild waters of the Parsnip. The work was utterly exhausting because the farther upriver they advanced, the stronger the current became. Poling was often the only method of making progress because the Parsnip was overflowing with spring runoff, and the banks of the river were so heavily lined with trees that it was impossible to use a tow line. Sometimes the men could only maintain a forward motion of sorts by pulling on the branches of partly submerged trees.

All the time the river level kept rising. On June 4, after embarking at four in the morning, it was nine in the evening before Mackenzie found a place to camp. Even then it was only a bank of gravel "of which little more appeared above water than the spot we occupied." In the morning they awoke to find the canoe and all its baggage half-sunk in the water, which had continued to rise during the night. Nothing could have discouraged the men more. Since leaving Fort Fork they had been witnessing the steady deterioration of their craft. It was no longer enough to gum the seams every night. By this time the canoe had to be extensively patched to keep up with the wear and tear inflicted on it by waters swollen and strengthened by spring rains.

On June 5, during part of which Mackenzie had left his party for several hours to view the country from a nearby height, they reported to him on his return that

the canoe had been broken, and that they had this day experienced much greater toil and hardships than on any former occasion. I thought it prudent to affect a belief of every representation that they made, and even to comfort each of them with a consolatory dram [of rum]. . . .

But Mackenzie does admit that the canoe had been reduced to "little better than a wreck" and had to be repaired extensively. To add to their miseries, the weather on the west side of the Rocky Mountains was much milder and "the gnats and mosquitoes appeared in swarms to torment us."

Eight days upstream from Finlay Forks Mackenzie became desperately anxious to find the carrying-place that the aged Beaver had said would take him to "the large river . . . where the inhabitants build houses and live upon islands." Although Mackenzie didn't know it, he had already missed the mouth of a waterway (the Pack) by means of which he could have got across to that river—probably because of his habit of indulging in a short doze in the canoe every now and again. Late that night, over a supper of boiled wild parsnips and pemmican, Mackenzie fretted about the location of the carrying-place. Had he missed it during one of his naps? Had he actually seen it and mistaken it for one of the numerous island channels on the river? Did it exist at all?

On June 9, in the course of another long day struggling upriver, the men smelled smoke and heard confused movements in the woods bordering the water. Two Sekani Indians emerged from the trees to brandish spears and make menacing gestures with bows and arrows. Mackenzie eagerly made for the river bank near them and ordered his men to pitch their tents and act normally as if making camp. He was determined not to lose this opportunity to gain whatever information he could.

It took the interpreters and Mackenzie quite some time to overcome the Indians' fear and distrust and convince them of the party's peaceful intentions, but the natives finally laid aside their weapons. "They examined us and everything about us with a minute and suspicious attention. They had heard, indeed, of white men, but this was the first time that they had ever seen a human being of a complexion different from their own." The two Sekani were joined by the others in their party— another man, three women, and seven or eight boys and girls. Mackenzie describes them as "low in stature, not exceeding five feet six or seven inches. . . . Their faces are round, with high cheek bones; and their eyes, which are small, are of a dark brown colour

. . . their hair is of a dingy black, hanging loose and in disorder over their shoulders, but irregularly cut in the front, so as not to obstruct sight . . . and their complexion is a swarthy yellow." He calmed their suspicions and "consoled" them with gifts of beads and other trifles. Noting that their food supply consisted entirely of dried fish, he even dipped into his precious pemmican rations and handed some around.

Although he succeeded in winning over these Sekanis, Mackenzie was surprised and puzzled by their answers to his questions. Despite the fact that they had obviously acquired a considerable amount of iron somewhere for spearheads, knives, and arrowheads, they said that they knew nothing of a great river to the westward. Yet there had to be a "chain of connection by which these people obtained their iron-work." Mackenzie promised to bring them vessels laden with goods and to arrange peace between them and their enemies, the Beaver Indians. Still they steadfastly denied any knowledge of a river that ran to the ocean. All they would admit to was trading for iron with a neighbouring band of Indians, who lived eleven days westward over a long carrying-place. These Indians travelled west for a whole moon to barter with tribes who, in turn, travelled farther west to the edge of the "Stinking Lake," where white men came in vessels "as big as islands." The Sekani were certain that the river that took them to that carrying-place was a branch of the Parsnip. Mackenzie began to suspect that his interpreters, who were as tired and discouraged as the voyageurs, were deliberately feeding him negative-sounding answers. "I therefore continued my attention to the natives, regaled them with such provisions as I had, indulged their children with a taste of sugar, and determined to suspend my conversation with them till the following morning."

The next morning, a Sekani was chatting with the party's Indian interpreters around the campfire. Mackenzie, standing nearby, understood enough of the conversation to realize that the Sekani was saying something about a great river that ran towards the midday sun and could be reached by going to the source of the Parsnip and then swinging west over three small lakes and three short portages. He quickly asked the Sekani to describe all this on a strip of bark with a piece of charred wood, which the man promptly did. Within an hour, the party was on its way upriver, Mackenzie having so impressed the Sekani that he had been induced to act as guide.

A day later they left the main stream of the Parsnip behind and traversed a two-mile-long body of water (Arctic Lake). A brief journal entry for June 12 notes that:

> We landed and unloaded, where we found a beaten path leading over a low ridge of land of eight hundred and seventeen paces in length to another small lake [Portage Lake].

In portaging these 817 paces to the second lake, Mackenzie and his followers had crossed the continental divide. They had left behind them waters draining ultimately into the Arctic. For the first time they were, in Mackenzie's words, "going with the stream." They were on water that would find its way to the Pacific Ocean.

Once across the third body of water (Pacific Lake) and the third portage, they came to a turbulent, ice-cold stream (James Creek), which Mackenzie would have good reason to name Bad River. In the course of the first day on its shallow, upper waters, they spent about as much time clearing away fallen trees and easing their craft over banks of gravel as they did canoeing. They had barely got under way the next morning when a surge of the current drove their craft sideways down the river and broke its back on a gravel bar. Driven on into deeper water by the stream's swift flow, the canoe was thrust against a large boulder, which shattered the stern. The violence of this contact hurled the craft across the river, where its bow was crushed by rocks.

> At this moment the foreman seized on some branches of a small tree in the hope of bringing up the canoe, but such was their elasticity that, in a manner not easily described, he was jerked on shore in an instant, and with a degree of violence that threatened his destruction.

Carried on over a cascade, the canoe had several large holes torn in it and many of its ribs broken. At Mackenzie's curt command, the crew tumbled out of the wreck into the water but held fast to the gunwales. Several hundred yards later, waterlogged but afloat, the canoe grounded in shallow water, and the badly shaken, half-frozen crew staggered to their feet. Somehow no one had been unjured, and the foreman turned up at that moment to help carry ashore the soaked, battered cargo.

Displaying his usual astuteness, Mackenzie first made sure that his men's spirits were revived: a roaring fire was built, a hearty meal eaten, and a generous slug of rum was drunk all round. Then he used his great powers of persuasion, appealing particularly to their loyalty and to their pride.

I brought to their recollection that I did not deceive them and that they were made acquainted with the difficulties and dangers they must expect to encounter before they engaged to accompany me. I also urged the honour of conquering disasters, and the disgrace that would attend them on their return home without having attained the object of the expedition. Nor did I fail to mention the courage and resolution which was the peculiar boast of the Northmen, and that I depended upon them, at that moment, for the maintenance of their character. ... At the same time I acknowledged the difficulty of restoring the wreck of the canoe, but confided in our skill and exertion to put it in such a state as would carry us on to where we might procure bark and build a new one.

His speech had the intended effect. One of the Indians found enough bark, poor in quality though it was, to patch up the worst gashes in their craft, and oilcloth was used to repair the minor holes. The job took two days. By the time they had finished, the canoe was held together almost as much by gum as by fabric.

They started off again on the clear, warm morning of June 15, plagued every step of their way by mosquitoes and sand flies. Mackenzie was careful to have twelve packs taken out of the canoe, and all but a crew of four portaged these along the bank of the creek. It took the party fourteen hours to travel three miles, but the canoe survived several dangerous places and remained afloat. That evening Mackenzie rewarded them with "the usual beverage which I supplied on these occasions." The next day they had to portage around several falls, first through a swamp, then in mud that was hip-deep, and finally through a seemingly endless tangle of fallen trees and thick underbrush. By seven in the evening Mackenzie and his followers had managed to advance two miles. To complete their miseries, the Sekani guide, who had been showing signs of deserting, stole away in the early hours of the next morning, despite the fact that Mackenzie and his second-in-command, Alexander McKay, took turns sitting up all night to keep an eye on him. This happened during McKay's watch, and Mackenzie was naturally displeased with him.*

June 17th was spent hacking a way back to the creek, floating the canoe downstream until large amounts of driftwood made this too dangerous, and then hauling everything along the banks of the river, which soon branched into various small, unnavigable channels. Once again they found themselves forced to carry the canoe and all its contents through swampy ground. But at eight in the evening, to their inexpressible joy, they came to the east bank of a navigable waterway. (The party had reached the headwaters of the Fraser between Herrick Creek and McGreg-

*It is not until his arrival at the Pacific that Mackenzie makes grudging admission of the services of Alexander McKay, although even this is only done in a footnote in the *Voyages*.

> It is but common justice to him, to mention in this place that I had every reason to be satisfied with his conduct.

Throughout the journal of the second voyage, mention of McKay is very casual, yet Mackenzie received faithful, steady support from his second-in-command. Mackenzie's attitude towards him is typically that of a Nor'Wester partner towards a clerk. With the possible exception of his friend, William McGillivray, who seems to have made a point of being courteous to all men, the wintering partners of the Company commonly displayed a brutal arrogance and condescension towards their immediate juniors and their other employees that was notorious even in an age that has been condemned by historians for its caste-conscious manners and habits.

or River.) By way of celebration, Mackenzie allowed his men to sleep in until seven in the morning, but by eight the party was afloat again on waters driven along by a strong current. That day they came to "the great fork, of which our guide had informed us" (the fork formed by the McGregor and Fraser Rivers).

Although his "Journal of A Second Voyage, &c." contains an astonishing amount of what Mackenzie calls "geographical details," many of which are compass directions for every mile or fraction of a mile he travelled, the notes of his journey down the Fraser River omit obvious landmarks. This was probably due to the early morning mists and the many rainstorms he encountered in the milder climate on the west side of the Rocky Mountains. However, he could not help but mention the portage around what we call the Prince George Canyon (about sixteen miles south of Prince George, B. C.): "The great body of water tumbling in successive cascades rolls through this narrow passage in a very turbid current, and full of whirlpools." About thirty-five miles farther on he describes another violent cascade (Cottonwood Canyon) that necessitated another laborious portage, although he reluctantly allowed four of his men to run the empty canoe down these rapids. He really had no option: the men were bone-tired and greatly disheartened by the collapse of the canoe in the course of the portage around the Prince George Canyon, an incident that cost them several hours of finicky, tedious repair work. The craft that was so light when they started out from Fort Fork that two men could carry it for three miles without resting was now too heavy to portage. Mackenzie had to admit that the canoe had now become so "crazy" that it was a matter of absolute necessity to construct another.

On June 21, somewhere about twenty miles below the junction of the Quesnel and Fraser Rivers (in the vicinity of modern Alexandria,* B. C.), Mackenzie landed to question some Salish Indians as to how best to get to the Pacific. As with the Sekani, he noticed that giving children sugar quickly loosened the tongues of their elders. The next day he did the same thing with

*Fort Alexandria, established here by the North West Company in 1821, was named after Mackenzie.

other Indians, and was intrigued enough by their frank, friendly reception to stay for a whole day of questions and answers. The following day, the twenty-third, after a restless night, he made the second major decision of the voyage, one as vital as his resolve to follow the Parsnip instead of the Finlay. Unfortunately, his decision, shrewd though it was in the circumstances, was based on a great deal of information and advice that was exaggerated and misleading.

It seemed obvious from all the replies he received from Indians that the river he was on ran south and that farther downstream there were three violent sets of falls and rapids that would be impossible for his party to run in a canoe already in an advanced stage of disintegration.

But besides the dangers and difficulties of the navigation, they added that we should have to encounter the inhabitants of the country, who were very numerous. They also represented their immediate neighbours [Shushwap Indians] as a very malignant race, who lived in large subterraneous recesses. [Their houses were built partly underground.] And when they were made to understand that it was our design to proceed to the sea, they dissuaded us from prosecuting our intention, as we would certainly become a sacrifice to the savage spirits of the natives.

Mackenzie sensed that much of this was exaggerated, if not erroneous. However, the accident of meeting an aged Shushwap seemed to confirm the navigational hazards farther down the river—this time they were said to be six in number—and the portages around them sounded as mountainous as the one he had made to avoid the Peace River Canyon. The fact that the old man could pinpoint these by drawing them on a large piece of bark greatly impressed Mackenzie. Even using this river route, the Pacific was still a long way off, which would make a return to Athabasca that year unlikely. But the Shushwap and some of his companions, many of them elderly men, described a promising cross-country route to the "Lake which the natives did not drink."

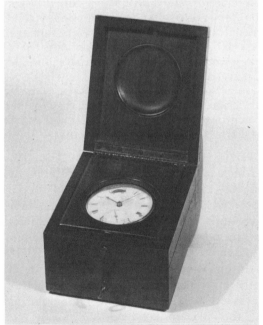

National Maritime Museum, London.

Where a modern surveyor following in Mackenzie's exploring footsteps would feel ill-equipped without a transit instrument, a chronometer, a telescope, a barometer, and an azimuth-theodolite, Mackenzie had to make do with a compass, a telescope, a box sextant, and a chronometer watch, all of which he bought in the course of a visit to London late in 1791. He went there because, on the voyage to the Arctic, "I was not only without the necessary books and instruments, but also felt myself deficient in the sciences of astronomy and navigation. I did not hesitate therefore to undertake a winter's voyage in order to procure the one and acquire the other."

The sextant and chronometer illustrated here, dated c. 1790, are most likely the type used by Mackenzie. The sextant (above) was used to establish the sun's altitude, a procedure normally performed each noon; then by referring to the tables of the sun's altitude in a nautical almanac and performing a simple calculation, Mackenzie would obtain a latitudinal reading. Longitude was much harder for him to establish since it basically depended upon knowledge of two times: that of his actual location (obtained from the position of the sun), and that of Greenwich, the prime, or zero, meridian of longitude. Unfortunately for Mackenzie, timepieces accurate to even one degree of longitude did not exist in his day, added to which he was trying to "carry" Greenwich time on his chronometer but forgot to wind it up on the night of July 6, 1793. However, he doesn't seem to have had much faith in his chronometer: he refers to it as his "achrometer" or "acrometer," employing a Greek prefix to emphasize the instrument's total lack of value as a timepiece.

Investigation of Mackenzie's survey work in 1793 suggests that, despite the crudity of his instruments, he was an exceptional observer; added to which he was careful to double-check his longitudinal readings by timing the eclipse of one or other of Jupiter's satellites and then referring to a set of astronomical tables. As a result, his greatest discrepancy is only one of forty miles, and he plots the upper Fraser within ten miles of its true position. If anything, Mackenzie distrusted his own ability as an observer and placed too much reliance on his estimates of distance and direction. A Canadian land surveyor who travelled and checked much of Mackenzie's route to the Pacific says of him, "He was too honest to 'fudge' his notes, so that by comparing his recorded latitudes and longitudes with his map in the Voyages *it is evident he tried to shift these so as to agree with his overestimate of distance."*

Alexander Mackenzie

They assured us that the road was not difficult, as they avoided the mountains, keeping along the low lands between them, many parts of which are entirely free of wood. According to their account, this way is so often travelled by them that their path is visible throughout the whole journey, which lies along small lakes and rivers. It occupied them, they said, no more than six nights to go to where they meet the people [Bella Coola Indians] who barter iron, brass, copper, beads &c. with them for dressed leather and beaver, bear, lynx, fox and marten skins. . . . They had been informed by those whom they met to trade with that the white people from whom these articles are obtained were building houses at the distance of three days' or two nights' journey [probably Nootka on Vancouver Island]. . . . With this route they all appeared to be well acquainted.

There were many matters for Mackenzie to consider in deciding which route to take. He only had provisions left for thirty days, and the sole food reserve was a ninety-pound bag of pemmican he had cached three days earlier. Supplementing this with game would be difficult because the party's supplies of ammunition were limited. In the course of the battering the canoe had received on James Creek, much of their stock of ball had been lost; the thirty pounds of shot ammunition now left could only be converted into bullets at a great waste of metal. Unless he could barter for food, or his Indian guides proved unduly skilful with bow and arrow, the party would have to go on short rations. Yet he was determined to return to Fort Chipewyan before winter set in. His Athabasca responsibilities awaited him and he could not ignore them.

An equally strong factor in his decision was his growing conviction that the river flowing past his encampment was not "Cook's River". He calculated that he should have come across it somewhere about 56°N, yet he was now just a little south of 52°N on a waterway that apparently ran far to the south. It was probably the "Great River of the West" he had heard of from so many Indians. (In later years he decided that it was the Columbia; it was, of course, the Fraser.) Thus he would have to backtrack and find the waterway he was to name the West Road

River* that, the Shushwap said, led to the "lake whose water is nauseous."

He addressed his men in a frank, determined manner, commending them on their "fortitude, patience and perseverance." But he stressed that he would reach the sea either by the overland journey to the west or, if guides failed to make this possible, by returning to where they now were and going downriver to its mouth, whatever the distance might be.

> At all events, I declared in the most solemn manner that I would not abandon my design of reaching the sea, if I made the attempt alone, and that I did not despair of returning in safety to my friends.

The self-control of the men had been slowly giving way to the fear and panic that in the wilderness meant death. But Mackenzie's continuous display of confidence and determination were, to his voyageurs, the only certain things in an uncertain world. His leadership was superb, and they responded to it by unanimously agreeing to follow wherever he might lead. In so doing, they paid him the finest of compliments.

Mackenzie found his guide, and the remainder of his westward journey is yet another example of his unshakeable will to reach the Pacific: the return some distance upriver in the "crazy vessel," which finally proved unrepairable and had to be replaced by building another from scratch; the westward climb into the cold, cloudy, blue-and-white world of the coastal mountains; the slogging march of almost two weeks through uplands sodden with rain and the meltwater of snow and ice; the descent into the lush, sheltered valley of Indians who worshipped and ate the salmon, the Bella Coolas; and on July 20 (in a borrowed Indian canoe) the arrival at the Pacific. Seventy-two days and twelve hundred miles out from Fort Fork, Mackenzie reached salt water at the mouth of the Bella Coola River.

On the last day or two of his journey to the coast,

*Known for many years since as the Blackwater River.

Preceding page:

At the lower left is the modern village of Bella Coola, located at the mouth of the river of the same name. Here Mackenzie at last reached Pacific waters. Far from showing elation of any kind, his journal entry that historic day is quite characteristically matter-of-fact, with perhaps a touch of melancholy to it at the end:

Saturday, July 20. We rose at a very early hour this morning . . . At about eight we got out of the river, which discharges itself by various channels into an arm of the sea [North Bentinck Arm]. The tide was out and had left a large space covered with seaweed. The surrounding hills were involved in fog . . . we saw a great number of sea-otters.

At two in the afternoon the swell was so high and the wind, which was against us, so boisterous, that we could not proceed . . . We therefore landed in a small cove . . . our stock was, at this time, reduced to twenty pounds of pemmican, fifteen pounds of rice, and six pounds of flour . . . among ten half-starved men, in a leaky vessel, and on a barbarous coast.

Leslie Kopas Photograph.

Mackenzie encountered some Bella Bella Indians. They were sullen and hostile, perhaps because of unscrupulous treatment by various American or Russian or British traders, who sailed up and down the coast seeking sea-otter pelts wherever they encountered bands of Indians. Mackenzie dealt with these Indians cautiously but firmly and so averted violence. But they pestered or shadowed him in their canoes for much of July 20 and 21, so he decided to camp for the night of the latter atop a large, steeply inclined rock face that plunges into the waters of a small cove or harbour(Elcho) on the north side of Dean Channel. After unsuccessful attempts to barter for a sea-otter fur with some aggressive Bella Bellas, Mackenzie and his men settled down for the night. They all had supper, although by this time "there was little of that, for our whole daily allowance did not amount to what was sufficient for a single meal." It was a fine moonlit night, and he ordered his men to keep watch by twos. Then he wrapped himself in his cloak and fell asleep.

On the clear, pleasant morning of the twenty-second, between fixing his position and quieting the fears of his men, who became quite nervous at the approach of two Bella Bella canoes,

> I now mixed up some vermilion in melted grease and inscribed in large characters, on the southeast face of the rock on which we had slept last night, this brief memorial— "Alexander Mackenzie, from Canada, by land, the twenty-second of July, one thousand seven hundred and ninety-three."*

By various observations during the day and night of the twenty-second, Mackenzie established his position as 128° 2′ West of Greenwich and 52° 20′ 48″ North. Then, and only then, did he give the word to McKay and the jittery, weary voyageurs to turn back eastward.

---

*The Historic Sites and Monuments Board of Canada has erected a monument and tablet to mark the terminus of his journey to the Pacific. The Board also had this famous inscription carved on the rock and filled with reddened cement.

In the Preface to the *Voyages* Mackenzie says that his second exploration was

> ... to determine the practicability of a commercial communication through the continent of North America between the Atlantic and Pacific Oceans, which is proved by my second journal.

He had proved exactly the opposite. No birchbark craft could survive the raging mountain waters he had traversed, least of all a canoe that would be laden to the gunwales with trade goods or bales of furs. Mackenzie had failed to find a practicable route to and from the Pacific through the confusing jumble of mountain ranges between the Rockies and the coast. But his characteristically stubborn refusal to accept defeat from man and nature alike made his failure seem like a triumph.

A Nor'Wester Agent

O n August 24, one month after starting back and three and a half months after beginning his voyage, Mackenzie and his men rounded a point of land jutting out into the Peace River and saw ahead of them the wooden walls of Fort Fork.

The return journey had not been without incident. At the start Mackenzie nearly lost his life when mobbed by Indians at a place he afterwards termed "Rascals' Village". He was saved by the accident of one of his voyageurs appearing on the scene, which caused the natives to flee. When the other men heard of the incident, most of them panicked. It took all of Mackenzie's patience, all of his logical reasoning, and all of his power of leadership to restore discipline. But this shaky beginning was more than offset by what they found when they had got back through the mountains to the junction of the West Road River and the Fraser. Their new canoe was intact where they had stored it; the pemmican they had cached was untouched, and other stores of provisions, hidden nearby, were all recovered. Game proved to be plentiful, particularly once they were back on the Peace. This was most fortunate, because on one occasion the carcass of a 250-pound elk lasted only three meals, being "consumed by ten persons and a large dog, who was allowed his share of the banquet." And, of course, although the same exhausting portages had to be made a second time, the eastward portion of the voyage was made over waters considerably lower and more manageable than those encountered on the outward trip.

Mackenzie's journal ends with the information that "after an absence of eleven months, I arrived at Fort Chipewyan, where I remained for the purposes of trade during the succeeding winter." It proved to be a bad season for him, a considerable letdown after being buoyed up by the various challenges of the Pacific voyage. This is confirmed by his correspondence with

Roderic, who was at another post. In January 1794, Mackenzie wrote his kinsman that

> . . . I am fully bent on going down [to Grand Portage]. I am more anxious now than ever. For I think it unpardonable in any man to remain in this country who can afford to leave it. What a pretty situation I am in this winter—starving and alone—without the power of doing myself or anybody else any service. The boy at Lac La Loche [Methye Lake], or even my own servant, is equal to the performance of my winter employment. . . .

He was quite right. A clerk could easily oversee the simple routine of a post in winter—inspecting stored packs of furs for signs of deterioration, dickering with the few Indians that arrived seeking a gun, ammunition, or rum on credit; or ensuring that the voyageurs were not lying half-asleep in their bunks, but were out in the bitter cold checking or mending the fishing nets. There were always wood-cutting parties to be organized, stores to be checked for pilfering, and many other minor housekeeping routines to be supervised. This petty, daily detail must have been utterly frustrating to a highly intelligent, ambitious man.

Worst still, Mackenzie's self-discipline was beginning to slip. By March he was confessing to Roderic that

> It is now the season in which I promised to write you and would wish that I could fulfil another promise I made you last fall and this winter. I need not say that I mean my Journal [of the Pacific voyage], which I wished you to peruse at your leisure and correct the calculations and other errors with that freedom due from one friend to another. Last fall I was to begin copying it, but the greatest part of my time was taken up in vain speculations. I got into such a habit of thinking that I was often lost in thoughts, nor could even write to the purpose. . . . I never passed so much of my time insignificantly, nor so uneasily. Although I am not superstitious, dreams among other things caused me much annoyance. I could not close my eyes without finding myself in company with the dead. I had some visions of late which

almost convinced me that I had lost a near relation or a
friend.

It was the latter end of January when I began my
work, thinking then I had time enough, though the reverse is
the fact, and I will be satisfied, and so must you, if I can
finish the copy to give you reading of it in the spring. I find
it a work that will require more time than I was aware of, for
it is not a quarter finished.

He had probably taken too much out of himself in the
summer of 1793 and was now paying the price of deep physical
exhaustion and of a serious mental depression that was largely the
result of the primitive, isolated life he had long hated. Yet, unlike
his colleagues in the trade, the normal diversions failed to ease
his situation. Many winterers made their existence tolerable by
steady or excessive drinking, but although he liked a dram every
now and then and could, on occasion, hold large amounts of
liquor, Mackenzie was not a great man for the bottle. Some
traders—Roderic was one—found comfort and solace in marriage
with an Indian girl, although most bourgeois simply bought a
mistress outright. Mackenzie took a chief's daughter to live with
him, yet there is no evidence that this was anything other than
a casual affair that had no emotional strength and brought him
no particular happiness. (A son, Andrew, was born to them and
later became a clerk in the Company in the Athabasca Department. He died in 1809 while quite young.) What Mackenzie
craved above all else was the civilized world beyond Athabasca,
specifically Montreal, where trade policies and decisions were
made. He had to be part of that world, and in 1794 he left Fort
Chipewyan with this intention firmly set in his mind. Only thirty
years old but a nine-year veteran of trade and travel in the pays
d'en haut, he had seen enough to confirm his suspicions that the
trade was still far too limited in scope and still too much of a
gamble. His thoughts were now concentrating on some kind of
overall management of the entire Canadian fur trade.

As it happened, Mackenzie was destined to leave the
pays d'en haut that year and never return farther west than Lake
Superior.

The explorer found a pleasant surprise awaiting him

when he came "out" with the Athabasca brigades and arrived at Grand Portage in the summer of 1794. No complaint was made about the wages and supplies that the Pacific expedition had cost the Company. Nor were there any grumbles that the exploration had not made practicable the immediate exploitation of new fur regions. Instead, he was complimented on displaying great fortitude in seeking new business, which was more and more becoming a prime objective of the Company. The Nor'Westers had had to take in several new members, which diminished share values and therefore made the Company anxious to increase annual returns. Competition, or rather an open threat of competition, had been levelled at the Nor'Westers, principally from the old Montreal firm of Todd, McGill & Co. and the new one of Forsyth, Richardson & Co., the Canadian subsidiary of a London fur company. When a formal agreement had been drawn up in 1792 in order to buy off Todd, McGill and Forsyth, Richardson by giving them a few shares, the explorer had been allotted no less than six shares in an expanded, forty-six-share North West Company.

The summer meeting of the partners that Mackenzie attended seems to have been full of argument and dissent. The new member firms, made wary by the outbreak of the French Revolutionary war in Europe and anxious to cut back trading operations in anticipation of a business slump, were very vocal about policy and operational methods. In addition, the sudden elevation the year before of William McGillivray—Mackenzie's friend from Isle-à-la-Crosse days—to a partnership in McTavish, Frobisher & Co., the dominating firm within the Company, caused rumblings of resentment among many of the more experienced winterers. McGillivray had served nine years in the pays d'en haut and was well liked and respected. Yet, as the nephew and protégé of the powerful Simon McTavish, he was the object of suspicion and distrust. Several wintering partners considerably senior to McGillivray were angry at being passed over by this promotion of a younger man. But all the winterers had one and the same thought: was the imperious, forceful McTavish, who, as senior agent, kept a tight grasp on the Company's purse strings and also dictated Company policies, going to groom a successor in his own image? Were they never to have a greater voice in their own business affairs?

The younger partners, too, among them Roderic and Simon Fraser, had a major grievance because they had been allowed only one share apiece under the agreement of 1792, despite McTavish's promises to do better by them.* They appealed to Mackenzie to present their case to higher authority for a doubling of their holdings. They also wanted him to get something done about the poor quality of certain trade goods recently supplied them. Firearms, in particular, had been so defective that Indians had refused to accept them as trading items.

Mackenzie successfully represented these complaints later in Montreal. Indeed, the way in which he worked out a detailed solution that was fair to these winterers (which included a willingness to release to them three of his own shares) became the basis of a further agreement in October, 1795. Mackenzie's name does not appear in the 1795 list of North West partners, except as "agent and Attorney" for the winterers. A few days after the document of agreement was signed, he was made a copartner and agent of McTavish, Frobisher & Company, which had become the virtual directorate of the North West Company. Mackenzie was now based at Montreal, the headquarters of the trade.

The Montreal to which Mackenzie returned was noticeably different from the town he had left nine years before. Within its ancient palisade, an eighteen-foot-high wall complete with loopholes and bastions, many of the old tin-roofed, rough-stone houses were being replaced by handsome buildings of carefully dressed limestone from local quarries. Near the river-front were one or two new warehouses, notably the large building occupied by McTavish, Frobisher just off Place Jacques Cartier. Montreal's population had increased to about six or seven thousand persons following an influx of United Empire Loyalists.

*Alexander Henry, that wily old Pedlar of the early days on Saskatchewan and Churchill waters, was another single-share partner. He had practically black-mailed the Company into giving him one forty-sixth of the profits as the price of his support and goodwill.

This circumstance, together with the wealth generated by the fur trade, had caused some of the town's richer members to look beyond its three main gates for a place of residence. The long-established Montreal habit of living over an office or shop was no longer good enough for them, and quite palatial homes had been built outside the town on the lower slopes of Mount Royal. One of these was James McGill's Burnside Manor on a "gentle-man's farm" of fields, gardens, and orchards on the southern flank of Mount Royal. Indeed some members of what has been called the "commercial aristocracy" had moved completely out of the Montreal area and were content with nothing less than a country residence, usually a seigneury. Others had retired to Scotland and there purchased large estates, where they lived the leisurely life of a "landed gentleman." If anything, the most spectacular change was just outside Montreal's east, or Quebec, gate, where a very busy brewery and distillery had been established by a Lincolnshire man named John Molson. But a few things had not changed. Montreal's streets remained narrow, unpaved, and badly lit; townspeople and farm folk still haggled daily in the principal market place; and, at certain times of the year, voyageurs could be heard carousing in the dingy taverns of the rue de la Capitale.

Thanks to his early years in the counting house of Finlay, Gregory & Company, Mackenzie was no stranger to many of the details of his new responsibility as agent. The entire business cycle of the Montreal trade revolved around the agents. Their prime duties were to import goods and export furs. The former were shipped to Montreal, and in the great warehouse of McTavish, Frobisher were stored

> . . . coarse woollen cloths of different kinds; milled blankets of different sizes; arms and ammunition; twist and carrot tobacco; threads, lines, and twine; common hardware; cutlery and iron-mongery of several descriptions; kettles of brass and copper, and sheet iron; silk and cotton handkerchiefs, hats, shoes, and hose; calicoes and printed cottons &c., &c., &c. Spirituous liquors and provisions are purchased in Canada [and were also imported from the West

Indies]. These and the expense of transport to and from the Indian country, including wages to clerks, interpreters, guides and canoemen, with the expense of making up the goods for the market, form about half the annual amount against the adventure. . . .

The "adventure"—the risky business of hauling goods and furs to and fro over six thousand miles of wilderness—certainly was expensive since the Company also had to feed, part-clothe, and pay

    . . . fifty clerks, seventy-one interpreters, one thousand one hundred and twenty canoemen, and thirty-five guides. Of these, five clerks, eighteen guides, and three hundred and fifty canoemen were employed for the summer season in going from Montreal to Grand Portage. . . .

Until the early years of the nineteenth century, the Company also fed at its own expense several hundred Indian women and children, the wives and families of the guides, interpreters, and voyageurs who wintered in the pays d'en haut.

    Each summer and winter was spent preparing for the dispatch of the following year's canots de maître to Grand Portage. There was the great labour of handling the goods that had been sent out from England in bulk as individual items but which had to be made up into assortments and then packed into ninety-pound pièces, the most economical unit of weight to paddle and portage into the pays d'en haut. Indian customers often had differing needs, and there were distinct local tastes or preferences even within a particular region, all of which had to be allowed for when making up the hundreds of packs of goods. McGillivray and Mackenzie had to supervise this entire operation very carefully. The paperwork was enormous, and the accounting was complicated because it also included provisions, clothing and other equipment, and a large payroll even by modern standards.

    There was, too, the accounting that dealt with the bales of furs received each fall at Montreal. According to Mackenzie:

In 1788, the gross amount of the adventure for the year did not exceed forty thousand pounds, but by the exertion, enterprise, and industry of the proprietors [wintering partners], it was brought in eleven years to triple that amount and upwards. . . .

All apart from the fact that the pelts of a particular animal varied in quality and had to be graded into several categories of fineness or coarseness, McTavish, Frobisher handled a total export of furs, which Mackenzie says was composed in 1798 of:

106,000	Beaver	6,000	Lynx
2,100	Bear	600	Wolverine
1,500	Fox	1,650	Fisher
4,000	Kitt Fox	100	Raccoon
4,600	Otter	3,800	Wolf
17,000	Musquash [musk rat]	700	Elk
32,000	Marten	750	Deer
1,800	Mink	1,200	Deer [dressed]

500 Buffalo robes, and a quantity of castoreum*

In addition to their day-to-day duties, McGillivray and Mackenzie had to fulfil their responsibilities as vital links between the import-export complexities of McTavish, Frobisher in Montreal and the far-flung activities of Nor'Westers in the pays d'en haut. The two men made the long journey to Grand Portage each summer to supervise the exchange of packs of goods for bales of furs. And at the depot there was the annual meeting with the wintering partners to discuss the state of the trade and to settle for the forthcoming year such matters as the location of employees, promotions, retirements, the continuance or abandonment of certain trading areas or the opening up of others, and other items of general policy.

While there was much work for the new agent to do,

*A glandular secretion of the beaver that was used as a fixative in the manufacture of perfume.

Montreal gave him ample opportunity to enjoy himself. He was now "Nor'West Mackenzie," a much-admired member of a group of people who delighted in giving numerous dinners or supper parties and used any excuse to organize dances and balls. One of his copartners, Joseph Frobisher, was host to many gatherings of notables, including some of the important military and administrative officials of what, in 1791, had become the Province of Lower Canada. The senior partner, Simon McTavish, probably the richest man in Montreal at this time, had recently married, set up house in rue Saint-Jean-Baptiste, and was much given to entertaining. It is reported that so many carriages rattled in and out of the arched gateway to the inner courtyard of his house that the nuns in the convent across the street could be heard voicing their disapproval. Mackenzie himself shared comfortable bachelor quarters with Will McGillivray in a house on the lower slope of Mount Royal. (One of their neighbours was John Gregory, Mackenzie's old associate from his early days in the trade, who was now a senior partner in McTavish, Frobisher.) Both men made up for the wintering years in which they ate dull food off tin plates and drank strong tea out of pewter mugs by purchasing fine china, cutlery, and glassware, hiring the services of a chef, and stocking large quantities of fine wines.

There is an irritating dearth of information on Mackenzie's private life at this time, although, unlike his earliest years, there are one or two snippets of information. Family papers confirm that he was the father of a daughter, Maria, born out of wedlock in Canada (Quebec). Was she a love-child or just the result of a casual affair? There is no indication, although the girl is known to have been brought up in Scotland by one of Mackenzie's sisters and, later on, married to a widower. And then there is a curious request some years later in a letter to the faithful Roderic. "I requested of you at parting to send fifty pounds to Mrs. Mackenzie of Three Rivers [Quebec] on my account, which I hope you will not neglect. This sum I mean to continue to her annually while Kitty remains single, and if I find that it is not sufficient with the support afforded her by her other friends, I can easily augment and continue it as long as I please. That young woman they have taken into their house must be in want of many

Of the four Beaver Club medals known to have survived, this one belonged to James McGill (1744-1813), the fur merchant and philanthropist who left his estate and £40,000 with which to establish what is now McGill University. Such a gold medal, worn suspended from a sky-blue ribbon, identified the wearer as a member of a very exclusive fraternity, established in 1785 by the same group of men who founded the North West Company. With the exception of a few honorary memberships, admittance was limited to those who had passed the test of at least one winter in the pays d'en haut and received a unanimous vote of acceptance by the members. One face of McGill's medal confirms that he first wintered as early as 1766.

The Club existed until 1817, although a brief unsuccessful attempt was made to revive it ten years later. There were no permanent premises, the meetings being held in various Montreal hotels. Members usually met twice a month between the first week in December and the second week in April. After a lavish meal, reported to be "bear, beaver, pemmican and venison served in the fashion of the posts," five formal toasts were rigidly observed: "The Mother of all Saints," "The King," "The Fur Trade in all its branches," "Voyageurs, Wives and Children," and "Absent members." Thereafter, the real drinking began. It is said that the group often reached such a degree of nostalgic intoxication that they engaged in a "grand voyage" by squatting in a long row on the floor and employing as paddles fire tongs, pokers, swords or walking sticks, all the while singing voyageur songs, which were sometimes interrupted by ear-piercing war whoops.

The list of members naturally reads like a history of the trade. Of the original 19, four—Charles Chaboillez, Maurice Blondeau, Hypolite des Rivières and Etienne Campeau—had made their first trip into Indian country before the fall of New France in 1760. Alexander Henry's claim to membership dates from 1761. All three Frobisher brothers are recorded. (Benjamin, who is not known to have been a winterer, must have wangled an honorary membership.) James Finlay, like McGill, dates from 1766 and Peter Pond from 1770. John Gregory's name appears in 1790 and that of William McGillivray in 1795. Roderic McKenzie was accepted in 1799 and Simon Fraser in 1803. Oddly enough, the name of Simon McTavish is not listed; there is no indication that he was ever made a member.

Alexander Mackenzie was elected to membership in 1795. Presumably his medal was lost, together with almost all his papers and possessions, in a fire that destroyed his house in Scotland some years after his death.

McCord Museum, Montreal.

necessaries to appear decently." The Mrs. Mackenzie he mentions may or may not have been a kinswoman. But who was Kitty? The mother of Maria? Another light-o'-love?

Luckily, we get a brief glimpse or two of a very companionable Mackenzie in these years of personal renown and increasing wealth. George Landmann, a lieutenant in the Royal Engineers who arrived in Montreal in 1797, records enjoying the hospitality of the bachelor duo. He had been barely twenty-four hours in Montreal before he was invited to every meal served in their house for the next few days. Landmann recalls one particular occasion.

> In those days we dined at four o'clock, and after taking a satisfactory quantity of wine, perhaps a bottle each, the married men. . . . and some others retired, leaving about a dozen of us to drink to their health. We now began in right earnest and true highland style, and by four o'clock in the morning, the whole of us had arrived at such a degree of perfection that we could all give the war-whoop as well as Mackenzie and McGillivray, we could all sing admirably, we could all drink like fishes, and we all thought we could dance on the table without disturbing a single decanter, glass or plate; but on making the experiment we discovered that it was a complete delusion, and ultimately we broke all the plates, glass, bottles, &c., and the table also; and worse than all, the heads and hands of the party received many severe contusions, cuts, and scratches. . . . [7]

Having promised to see him off on a trip to Quebec City, McGillivray and Mackenzie turned up at Landmann's hotel later that morning and made sure that he was in a reasonably fit state to travel.

Landmann also described the traditional meal for the "big bourgeois" (agents) before they set off for Grand Portage from Lachine, the historic embarkation point a few miles west of Montreal. On this particular occasion, McGillivray and Mackenzie were going to take Landmann part of the way with them and had invited him to join them in the Company's Lachine warehouse, where an "abundant luncheon" had been prepared. Landmann begins by observing that the military officers and Nor'Westers present were all from the Highlands of Scotland and that therefore he was the only *foreigner* present.

> Lunch was quickly eaten and the bottle had freely circulated, raising the old Highland drinking propensity, so that there was no stopping it. Highland speeches and sayings, Highland reminiscences, and Highland farewells, with the dioch and dorich [deoch-an-doris], over and over again, was kept up with extraordinary energy, so that by six or seven o'clock I had, in common with many of the others, fallen from my seat. To save my legs from being trampled on, I continued to draw myself into the fireplace and sat up in one of the corners, there being no stove or grate. I there remained very passive, contemplating the proceedings of those who still remained at the table. . . . Mackenzie as president and McGillivray as vice-president were the last retaining their seats. Mackenzie now proposed to drink to our memory and then give the war-whoop over us, fallen foe or friends, all nevertheless on the floor, and in attempting to push the bottle to McGillivray, at the opposite end of the table, he slid off his chair and could not recover his seat. Whilst McGillivray, in extending himself over the table in the hope of seizing the bottle which Mackenzie had attempted to push to him, also in like manner began to slide on one side, and fell helpless on the floor.[8]

The drinking spree at Lachine took place in May 1798. Mackenzie was then thirty-four, financially comfortable, one of Montreal's better-known figures, and something of a hero to many of the younger wintering partners in the North West Company. But he was happy with neither his position nor his prospects in McTavish, Frobisher & Co. He was the fifth of five copartners and had little say in determining overall Company policy. A long-cherished plan he had to expand, regulate, and control the entire fur trade had not been advanced one whit. In addition, he must have been greatly disturbed by the reports of increasing numbers of American traders enjoying both the sea-otter trade of the Pacific coast and the money to be made on these pelts in Chinese ports. His own copartners seemed to be blind to the huge profits in the China trade, one end of which began under their very noses. McTavish, Frobisher leased a warehouse in rue Vaudreuil to John Jacob Astor, a stolid, unassuming German immigrant and resident of New York City, who came each year to Montreal to buy Canadian furs and retailed them in the eastern United States and also in Canton, China. Mackenzie's associates seemed slow to appreciate Astor's Asian market, which earned him thousands of dollars annually. Indeed, other than Mackenzie, only that sharp-eyed speculator, Alexander Henry, appeared to see what Astor was up to. Henry was quick to befriend and enter into partnership with him and always made sure that Astor stayed at the Henry house in rue St Urbain during his annual visits to Montreal.

Mackenzie seems to have excited his friend and colleague, Will McGillivray, with his notions of establishing "one common interest" to supervise the trade and to conduct all freighting of goods through Hudson Bay. Mackenzie had even impressed these same ideas on Colonel John Graves Simcoe, Lieutenant Governor of Upper Canada, as early as 1794, the year in which he had left the pays d'en haut. On his way to Montreal, Mackenzie stopped off at Niagara to pay his respects to the governor, and they had a long chat together. Simcoe judged him "as intelligent as he is adventurous," listened attentively to his proposals, which included the establishment by the British government of two posts on the Pacific coast as a claim to sovereignty, and incorporated these proposals in a long report on western problems that he sent to London. In Simcoe's account is the first intimation of the project that Mackenzie tried to promote over and over again in later years.

> . . . the most practicable Rout to the Northwest was thro' the territories of the Hudson's Bay Company; that by the Rout from Great Britain all the Navigation from Montreal thro' the chain of Lakes & their immense Communication to the most distant part of the interior Country & its consequent Carriage would be saved.[9]

Nothing came of Simcoe's report, and in succeeding

years, probably in the course of several visits to England, Mackenzie learned why. His plan of action ran counter to the interests of three, well-established commercial monopolies. First, the Hudson's Bay Company possessed by royal charter the exclusive powers of trade and government in those regions whose waters emptied into Hudson Bay, which amounted to the entire pays d'en haut excepting Athabasca. While the Company could not oust the Montrealers from the western interior, it did deny them the use of the Bay. Second, the East India Company had a similar charter for much of India, but also possessed the exclusive right of British trade in China, an obvious market for sea-otter and other furs. (One of Mackenzie's few satisfactions in 1798 was acting as the Company's representative in New York City, where he successfully negotiated with Astor to ship furs to China using Astor's facilities and vessels as a cover. The astute Astor had personally managed to wangle a special permit from the governor of the East India Company to trade freely in any Company port in India or China.) The third monopoly belonged to the South Sea Company, which had the right of trade west of Cape Horn. No British vessel could trade beyond the Cape without Company permission, which could only be secured by paying a special toll.

Unfortunately, even McGillivray had been unable to promote Mackenzie's grand design within McTavish, Frobisher. Once more competition had been steadily building up in the pays d'en haut and had completely absorbed the day-to-day attention of Mackenzie's copartners. This time, the opposition to the North West Company refused to be bought off, and the Nor'Westers found themselves facing competent rivals all the way from Grand Portage to Fort Chipewyan.

In 1787 the Nor'Westers had absorbed Gregory, McLeod & Company, Mackenzie's old firm. After that, most of the independent traders or fur houses who showed up northwest of Grand Portage were usually intimidated and induced to work to the southwest. If they were big enough, they were pacified with a few, well-paying, North West Company shares. As for the Hudson's Bay Company, with a policy of dependence upon Indian middlemen it stood no chance against the "wolves of the north"; the Nor'Westers were able to bribe or bully so many

John Jacob Astor (1763-1848) was born near Heidelberg, Germany. After a brief apprenticeship in his brother's musical-instrument business in England, sixteen-year-old Jacob decided to try out the same occupation in North America with a small amount of stock bought from his brother. However, the accident of meeting and taking employment with a fur merchant in New York City changed his plans. Astor became so intrigued by the steady public demand for beaver hats that he decided to study the British and European fur markets very carefully, The demand for pelts he uncovered was so great that by 1786 he was back in the United States in business for himself. By 1800 Astor was shipping thousands of furs annually to London, England, via Montreal (to avoid the British tariff on U. S. goods).

A short, stocky, stolid-looking man with a marked Teutonic accent, Astor was often patronized or ignored by his fellow fur merchants, American and British alike. They would have done well to follow where he led. Not content with a European market, Astor also engaged in trade with merchants in Canton, China, where pelts could be sold for prices several times higher than those offered in Britain or Europe.

Although Astor built up a fortune largely from land investment and speculation in and around New York City, it is as a fur merchant that he is best remembered. Astor was a master of that trade. He could think in terms of continental and world trade just as perceptively as Alexander Mackenzie. Astor sought not only to outsell the North West Company but every other Montreal fur merchant into the bargain: using the westward trail to the Pacific blazed by Lewis and Clark, he intended to establish fur posts at intervals along that trail but, above all, to secure its strategic western end, the mouth of the Columbia River. With this purpose in mind he organized the American Fur Company and its offshoot, the Pacific Fur Company, with its base at Fort Astoria on the south bank of the Columbia estuary.

Astor nearly succeeded in monopolizing the fur trade of the entire Pacific Northwest and a highly lucrative trade in sea-otter pelts with China. Had it not been for the War of 1812, which the Nor'Westers used as an excuse to grab Astoria, he probably would have accomplished what he planned. As it happened, Astor's actions produced a rich political dividend that Mackenzie sought for Britain. In building Fort Astoria four months before David Thompson reached the Pacific via the Columbia, Astor gave the United States a claim to what came to be called the Oregon Territory. By 1846, the westward movement of the American people had

progressed as far as the Pacific coast. In the diplomatic negotiations that settled formal ownership of the Pacific coast that year, the U. S. government was able to claim territory as far north as the 49th parallel, which made the lower Columbia River and the Oregon Territory part of the U. S. A.

Astor had the luck to arrive in North America at a time when the economy of the United States was expanding with great rapidity. With his driving ambition to acquire riches, his habit of combining foresight with hard work, and his ability to cozen knowledge and information out of others—notably his Montreal friend, Alexander Henry—it is not surprising that when he died he was the richest man in the United States. His New York City mansion, Astor House, was a forerunner of family hotel properties that much later included the Astor Hotel and the Waldorf-Astoria.

Indians into becoming their customers that HBC dividends, after years of yielding a 10 per cent return, dropped to 8 per cent and towards the end of the century sank to four. The Nor'Westers did not even suffer any inconvenience from the not-too-precise boundary agreement in 1783 between Great Britain and the newly established republic of the United States, although the agreement placed Grand Portage six miles within American territory and threatened to debar British subjects from trading anywhere south and west of the Great Lakes. Thanks in large part to persistent lobbying by the fur merchants of Montreal in Quebec City and also in London, British garrisons had been maintained in the Great Lakes region. In effect, this guaranteed the continuance of pre-1783 conditions. And since American officials and military men were too busy safeguarding the first settlers in the new western territories between the Appalachian Mountains and the Mississippi, or battling with pro-British Indians, those Montrealers who had long engaged in the southwest trade continued to do so. Thus, in the period from 1787 to 1795, the Nor'Westers were only too happy to monopolize the Northwest trade to the best of their very considerable abilities. But after this period their monopoly was challenged by other Montrealers.

Having by 1794 finally subdued the Indians, the administration of President George Washington took a hard line with the British government. Washington and his colleagues insisted that, by 1796, all redcoat garrisons in the Great Lakes region—which included the vital supply centres of Detroit and Michilimackinac—be evacuated, a demand that was formally agreed to in what is known as Jay's Treaty (1794). Since it seemed possible that the American government might not allow British subjects to continue to enjoy the diminishing, but still considerable, Great Lakes fur trade, this reversal of the status quo in the southwest trade suddenly caused some Montreal fur merchants to have sobering, second thoughts about their involvement in that trade. They had large capital investments in warehouses, goods, and employees. But what would they do with all these investments if harassed by American customs regulations and forced to pay duties on goods imported into and furs exported from the United States? (Which was exactly what did, in time, occur.) The result was that, first, one, and then a second well-financed Montreal fur house began to compete with the Nor'Westers in the pays d'en haut. This turn of events affected the careers of many men, but especially that of Alexander Mackenzie.

In the last decade of the eighteenth century the three giants of the Canadian fur trade were the North West Company, Todd, McGill & Company, and Forsyth, Richardson & Company (the latter two directed, as might be expected by Scots). Among them, they accounted for close to two-thirds of all furs exported from Montreal. But at the time of a further North West Company reorganization in 1795 Todd, McGill had decided against engaging actively in the northwest trade. Forsyth, Richardson, a firm that was gradually withdrawing from the southwest trade, found its proposed share of the arrangement of 1795 unacceptable and fought back by providing financial backing for various free traders in the pays d'en haut. One of them was Mackenzie's namesake and nephew who, like Roderic, spelled his name "McKenzie." A one-time Detroit trader, he eventually joined forces with several other winterers—of whom some were experienced Nor'Westers—and in 1798 signed a formal agreement with Forsyth, Richardson and the firm of Leith, Jamieson & Company (two more Scots who were pulling out of the southwest trade) to serve the "New North West Company" or, as it was usually called by the Nor'Westers, the XY Company.* By 1799, this opposition had penetrated as far inland as Lake Athabasca and set up a trading post near Fort Chipe-wyan.

Several historians have implied that Mackenzie had some hand or other in creating the XY group, although there is no proof that he was running with the hares and hunting with the hounds. He seems to have been aware of what was develop-ing. He wrote Roderic in October 1797 of "the formation of a concern against the North West Compy. by Messrs. Forsyth,

*The reason the Nor'Westers almost always referred to the opposition as the XY Company seems to be that, from the start, the bales, kegs, and pièces of the Company bore the brand XY, just as those of the older Company bore the shipping label NW.

Richardson & Company and others," a statement that anticipated by a year the actual legal establishment of the New North
West Company. However, this sounds very much like trade
gossip. It was not until he wrote his Montreal colleagues in June
1799 from Grand Portage that Mackenzie seems to have gathered
any positive information regarding the opposition's corporate
structure and personnel. This letter clearly reads as if he had just
found out the first detailed information about the XY Company.

> . . . This company consists of 20 shares, 12 of which
> are held by Forsyth, Richardson & Company, and Leith,
> Shepherd & Company, formerly merchants of Detroit, but
> now of Montreal. Those shares are to supply a capital as it
> may be required in goods and money to carry on the business
> but at no time to exceed £30,000. . . . The other 8 shares
> are to be, or are already given to people for transacting the
> business in Canada and this country [the pays d'en haut] as
> partners and give their labour in lieu of share of stock. Mr.
> [Daniel] Sutherland [an ex-Nor'Wester] has one of them as
> Montreal Agent, Mr. [George] Sharp [an ex-Detroit trader]
> one as Grand Portage agent . . . Alexr. McKenzie [his
> nephew] and [John] McDonald from Detroit each a share as
> wintering partners. . . . .
> Peronne and Mezier La Haye are the only ones
> [clerks] that ever wintered above [Sault] St. Marie. They have
> some others but of no note. Their North guides are Roy
> Boucanné and Pierre Jollie the Drunkard, both well known to
> most of you. They had Marsolet, but he finished his voyage
> in this world a few days before I left Montreal, and you pay
> your share of 2 dollars which we gave the priest for allowing
> him to begin his journey in the next. . . .

There were only fourteen shares in the XY Company
at this time, of which three were held by Forsyth, Richardson and
three by Leith, Jamieson & Company, and the corporate worth
was valued at $20,000. However, Mackenzie was correctly
informed as to the various other pieces of information he
supplied.
Mackenzie had no reason at this time to change sides.

The XY Company had just started to challenge the "wolves of the north." Others had tried and failed to upset the near monopoly of trade that the Nor'Westers enjoyed in the pays d'en haut. All that is known about Mackenzie at this point in his career is that, in October 1799, he sailed for England aboard the merchantman *Desire*, although his contract with McTavish, Frobisher was due for renewal in December of that year.

Sir Alexander Mackenzie

*I*n the long history of the fur trade, there are few more puzzling episodes than the break in 1799 between Alexander Mackenzie and McTavish, Frobisher & Company. No conclusive explanation is to be found in any contemporary correspondence or other record that has survived. Even Roderic fails to provide a reason, his only comment being the cryptic one that neither Mackenzie nor McTavish, Frobisher felt inclined to discuss a new contract "owing to an unfortunate misunderstanding between Mr. Mackenzie and Mr. McGillivray so that they cannot act well together." As for the cousins' long habit of correspondence, this lapsed for some years and reveals nothing except that on Mackenzie's side relations became positively frosty. After an unsuccessful attempt to detach his kinsman from service with the Nor'Westers, the "Dear Roderic" and "Dear Rory" of earlier letters becomes "Dear Sir."

Much gossip and speculation attended the departure from the trade and from Canada of "Nor'West Mackenzie." John George McTavish, like McGillivray a Simon McTavish protégé, wrote to his brother that Mackenzie wanted his name to appear in that of the firm. John George also remarked that when Mackenzie failed to get this concession, he immediately proposed that he be made senior to McGillivray when transacting business at the summer meeting of the partners and was again refused by Simon McTavish. Alexander Henry noted in a letter to an old Detroit friend and fur-trade associate that

> ...the old N West Company [and] Fraser & Company [the London branch of McTavish, Frobisher] is all in the Hands of McTavish, and McKensey [sic] is out, the latter went off in a pet, the cause as far as I can learn was who should be first—McTavish or McK. and as there could not be two Caesars in Rome one must remove.[10]

A common view of the parting of the ways is that

Mackenzie was the young, daring agent who ran afoul of Simon McTavish, the aging, conservative senior member of the firm. Mackenzie, the theory goes, was the eager advocate of expanding trade via a cheap Hudson Bay freight route and also reaching out for the China trade; McTavish resented any plan that would diminish the role of Montreal in the trade. Like so many stark black-and-white judgments, this one does not stand up very well under close examination.

It is probably true, as several reports have it, that McTavish became short-tempered and increasingly dictatorial in his latter years. Certainly many of the wintering partners, who felt that he had grown careless of their interests and was far too concerned with the Montreal and London ends of the business, were quick to resent his haughty manner and often referred to him as "The Marquis." On the other hand, McTavish did have the good sense to leave their affairs largely in the hands of McGillivray and Mackenzie while he tried, through McTavish, Fraser, & Company—his London subsidiary—to market the furs they obtained, furs that could no longer be easily sold in a Britain and Europe distracted by the French Revolutionary war.

However, Mackenzie was not the only one who was eager to exploit new markets. Until his sudden death in 1804, McTavish remained as expansion-minded as he was when he started out in the trade. While it is only possible to speculate that he may have been one of the "four interests" that Alexander Henry reported in 1775 as struggling to capture the trade of the Saskatchewan and as having "joined their stock together," it is known that he was one of the few merchants investing money in the pays d'en haut at that time. He was very probably the grey eminence behind the North West Company arrangements of 1779 and 1783, which quickly exploited Pond's extension of the trade all the way north and west into Athabasca. In the early 1790s, perhaps sensing the way American political winds were beginning to blow, McTavish attempted further expansion. He tried (without success) to lease transit rights through the Bay from the Hudson's Bay Company. He began to market furs in China by freighting them out of Boston on ships bought by the Company, an extremely unprofitable venture until, in the late

Simon McTavish (1750-1804) was born in Scotland, immigrated to North America at the age of thirteen, and probably found employment as an apprentice to a fur merchant in Albany or Detroit. Despite the fact that McTavish became one of the most successful individuals in the fur trade and was quite likely the richest man in turn-of-the-century Montreal, we know more about his achievements than we do about the man himself. What little personal information there is has been found in his correspondence with a friend in Detroit during the period 1774 to 1779. Thus we learn that McTavish loved "good wine, good oysters, and pretty girls," was "like a fish out of water when not in love," possessed a somewhat mischievous sense of humour, and delighted in scandalous chat and gossip. These letters also make it clear that he was hard-working, his business dealings taking him regularly from New York City to Montreal to Michilimackinac to Grand Portage.

McTavish was far-seeing, too. At first he appears to have engaged in the trade of the lower Great Lakes region at the supply point of Albany. But when the British Government's Quebec Act of 1774 annexed large tracts of Indian territory, he soon made Montreal his base of operations and the pays d'en haut his special business concern. He seems to have sensed that the future of the fur trade lay in the pays d'en haut.

The only other source of information on the character of Simon McTavish is his will. He made generous provision for his wife, children, and all his immediate relatives. However, not only did he leave large sums of money to several friends and godchildren but set aside £1000 for the purpose of "assisting such of my poor relatives in Scotland as I may have neglected to provide for." The will also included an amazing clause that implies a kindly nature:

I give and bequeath to the surviving children of William Kay, late of Montreal, aforesaid, merchant, deceased, the sum of one thousand pounds current money aforesaid, as I am doubtful whether I was justly entitled to the amount of the judgement rendered in my favour in the court of Appeals in this province against the Estate of the late William Kay, respecting the property of the late David McCrae.

Public Archives of Canada.

1790s, he agreed to cut costs to some extent by using John Jacob Astor as a shipping agent. And in 1800, McTavish would autho-rize the dispatch of William McGillivray's brother Duncan, and David Thompson, the Company's "astronomer and surveyor," to find a way through the Rocky Mountains to the Pacific coast.

McTavish's plans for expansion may well have included Mackenzie's two voyages.

A clue to this comes from the pen of that doughty, Aberdeen-born clergyman, John Strachan. Long before he acquired prominence as prelate and politician, Strachan managed to keep up with much that was going on in the slowly developing provinces of Upper and Lower Canada, including, of course, various doings of note in the fur trade. When he immigrated to Upper Canada as a tutor in 1799, the trade was far and away the most important single industry in British North America. And with typically Scots foresight and prudence, Strachan stopped off at Montreal for a few days to make himself known to the town's Scottish church and community, many of whom were fur merchants. (In 1807, Strachan married the widow of Andrew McGill, one such merchant, and became a friend and adviser to her brother-in-law, James McGill, who was a man of considerable repute in the trade.) In 1802, Strachan was living in Cornwall, a small community a few miles west of Montreal, where he was trying to establish a school. In the middle of relay-ing bits and pieces of local news to Dr. James Brown, an old friend and confidant in Scotland, Strachan suddenly remarks,

You have no doubt seen McKinsie's [Mackenzie's] voyage across the continent, which settles the long disputed North West Passage in the negative. He is a man of great intrepidity and considerable presence of mind. But the praise he acquired, tho' not diminished, should be extended to some of his Mercantile associates, particularly to a Mr. McTavish, the first merchant in the two provinces were it generally known that he was the original projector, and pushed it [exploration] forward. Nor did he want the ability for putting it into execution, but he could not be spared from conducting the business of the company. McKinsie and he have quarrelled about their mercantile enterprises, which probably prevented him [McTavish] from such a portion of praise as his connexion with the voyage most justly merited.[11]

Another clue that credits McTavish was recorded by yet another Scot, Thomas Douglas, fifth Earl of Selkirk, who visited Upper and Lower Canada in 1803/04. In the course of a brief stay in Montreal, Lord Selkirk met and chatted with "most of the grandees, nabobs, of the N. W. Co.," and several of their trade colleagues, one of whom was Isaac Todd. Todd was a veteran Montreal fur merchant. He was outfitting traders in the pays d'en haut at least as early as 1770, had been one of the original North West Company partners in 1779, and was now the senior partner of the firm of Todd & McGill. (His copartners were Andrew and James McGill.) His corporate interests lay in the Lake Michigan and upper Mississippi regions, which may account for Selkirk's remark that Todd "seems almost the only man who has maintained a constant friendly intercourse with both parties [Nor'Wester and XY executives]." (This may have been one reason why Mackenzie sent Todd an autographed copy of the *Voyages*.) At any rate, Todd remarked to Selkirk that Sir Alexander Mackenzie was guilty of "unfair private conduct towards them [Nor'Wester management] as well as misrepresentations in his book—he has certainly been unfair in not stating that it was McT. [McTavish] who planned both his expeditions. . . . "[12]

Now, Todd's remarks may have been nothing more than table talk of a somewhat biased nature. After all, he and McTavish were friends of long standing. Yet there are several intriguing pieces of circumstantial evidence that suggest that what Strachan told Brown and what Todd said to Selkirk may well have been true.

As noted earlier, the manuscript of the 1789 expedition, the only part of the *Voyages from Montreal* where Mackenzie's writing is clearly separable from William Combe's additions, is entitled "Journal of a Voyage performed by Order of the N. W. Company, in a Bark Canoe in search of a Passage by Water through the N. W. Continent of America from Athabasca to the Pacific Ocean in Summer 1789." In the *Voyages from Montreal*, there is no mention of "by Order of the N. W. Company." The title is simply "Journal of a Voyage, etc."

Second, several of Mackenzie's biographers say or imply that, initially, he kept his intention to explore northward in 1789 secret from everyone except Roderic. Yet a letter Mackenzie sent to Grand Portage to the agents of the North West Company twelve days before he set off on his first voyage implies that Messrs. McTavish and Frobisher knew he was going off exploring. In this communication, he expresses concern that he might not be back in time to make certain Cree Indians resume the hunt for beaver in the winter, mentions a potential summer trade with Yellowknifes and Slaves on the west side of Great Slave Lake, and adds, "I intend to pass that way on my voyage for a supply of provisions." This brings up a matter that has often been overlooked: Mackenzie's voyages were made on Company time and at Company expense.

Nor'Wester management had long been committed to expanding the trade of the pays d'en haut and, of course, to securing a firm monopoly of it. In the 1780s, a period when the line the international boundary should follow west of the Great Lakes and occupation of military posts in and around the lakes was being argued back and forth between British and American officials, many a clever Company argument urged authorities in Quebec to grant preferential treatment. Only Nor'Wester wintering partners, it was claimed, knew the strategic routes of the "Indian country" beyond the Great Lakes. Only the resources and the activities of the Company, it was claimed, would offset the dangers of Americanization of the pays d'en haut. It was pointed out that, thanks to the great efforts made by Nor'Westers, there was a continuous Indian market for British goods that would "Promote the Commercial Interest of the Province." And government was also reminded that the Company had sought to explore a way across the continent to tap the lucrative sea-otter trade and, at the same time, offset Russian claims to the North Pacific coast.

One set of arguments was beautifully contradictory, although written in very polite, highly-respectful terms. Addressed in 1784 to Governor Haldimand by Benjamin and

Joseph Frobisher, close business associates of McTavish and as commercially-minded a pair of Yorkshiremen as ever walked this earth, the memorandum[13] is an excellent example of business logic and Company propaganda. In one particular paragraph, Nor'Westers are described as seeking "to obtain a perfect knowledge of the country, without interfering with the Commercial rights of the Hudson's Bay Company, which on all occasions they will carefully avoid." A few lines later, on the grounds that the Nor'Westers would explore and extend the pays d'en haut, his Excellency the Governor is requested "to extend to the Company your Favour and protection to obtain for them an Exclusive Right [for ten years] to the trade of the North-west." (Which would not avoid but completely void the commercial rights of the Hudson's Bay Company!) As Peter Pond bluntly, and somewhat immodestly, put it in 1785 in the memorandum[14] that accompanied his second map of the Northwest,

> Your Memorialist begs leave to assure your Honour [Henry Hamilton, Haldimand's successor as governor of Quebec] that the persons connected in the North West Company are able and willing to accomplish the important discoveries proposed. . . . having men among them who have already given proof of their genius and unwearied industry in exploring these unknown regions as far as the longitude of 128 degrees west of London . . . and the Company will procure at its own expense such assistants as may be found necessary to pursue the work already begun, until the whole extent of that unknown country between the latitudes of Fifty Four & Sixty Seven to the North Pacific Ocean is thoroughly explored . . . by which means so firm a footing may be established as will preserve that valuable trade from falling into the hands of other powers [Russia and the United States]: and under proper management, it [the trade] may certainly in a short time be so extended as to become an object of great importance to the British Nation. . . .

Pond ends on the usual Nor'Wester note of high moral purpose. He hopes that his Honour will give the memorandum

> . . . all the support in Your Power in order to obtain for the Company an exclusive right to the trade to the North West of Lake Superior for the space of Ten Years only as a reward for the toil and expence [sic] of such an arduous and public Spirited Enterprise. . . .

By 1790, Nor'Wester lobbying had made itself felt all the way to the top of the official ladder. Late that year, Guy Carleton, governor-in-chief of British North America, wrote to a British cabinet minister, enclosing with his letter[15] "a sketch of the North Western parts of this Continent, communicated by Peter Pond, an Indian trader from this province, showing his discoveries, the track pursued, and the stations occupied by him and his party, during an excursion of several years, from which he returned in 1788. . . . Mr. McTavish, one of the principal partners of that Company who has lately sailed from hence for London, will be able to give such information concerning Mr. Pond's Map, and the Country resorted to by their Agents, as may be required."

Mackenzie himself comes close to admitting that his explorations were a continuance of the Company's expansionist policy. On the first page of the Preface to the *Voyages* he remarks on

> . . . the practicability of penetrating across the continent of America. . . . The general utility of such a discovery has been universally acknowledged; while the wishes of my particular friends and commercial associates that I should proceed in the pursuit of it, contributed to quicken the execution of this favourite project of my own ambition.

The "wishes of his friends and commercial associates" is suggested by events in 1792, the year immediately preceding the dash to the Pacific. As noted earlier, Mackenzie spent the winter of 1791/92 in London mastering the techniques of surveying. He sailed for Montreal in May 1792, reached Fort Chipewyan in October and, in November, the site of Fort Fork on the Peace River, *where men had been busy since the spring of '72 felling and trimming timber with which to build a wintering post.* (There is no indication anywhere that Mackenzie conceived the idea of an advance base for the Pacific expedition. But even if he had, wouldn't it have had to be approved by management?) Doesn't it seem logical that Mackenzie was given leave of absence to improve his navigational skills and that, in his absence, management made arrangements whereby he could employ these skills as soon as possible after he returned to Athabasca?

It will be remembered that Mackenzie fails to acknowledge his geographical debt to Peter Pond. And in the *Voyages*, Mackenzie would have us believe that he set off on the exploration of 1789 to settle "the dubious point of a practicable North-West passage" and that his second exploration determined "the practicability of a commercial communication through the continent of North America." Each of these statements is something less than truthful. Is it, then, very surprising that he would omit to mention executive initiation, approval, and encouragement of his explorations?

No, Mackenzie was definitely not the only one who was eager to exploit new markets. So why then did he part company with McTavish, Frobisher?

There is a strong possibility that the rift between Mackenzie and Simon McTavish was not as simple as youth versus age or, as has been suggested, because of disagreement over corporate policy. It is true that Mackenzie disliked the Company's expensive connection with Astor. Letters written by him during the three months he spent in New York City in 1798 reveal that he was extremely concerned about the costs of using American ports and shipping facilities. And it is also true that Mackenzie was utterly convinced the future of the trade lay in a transport route through Hudson Bay, not via Montreal. Despite all this, a more likely explanation for the break between the two men is the thrust of Mackenzie's ambition to get to the top, where he could make major decisions and implement them. There are hints of this in contemporary reports, none of which can be substantiated; but they suggest that Mackenzie was impatient with his junior-partner status in a firm in which McGillivray was being groomed for executive office.

The first hint is in McGillivray correspondence. A boon companion of Mackenzie, he was presumably in a position to know something of his friend's private thoughts. McGillivray wrote in the fall of 1799 to Aeneas Cameron, a fellow Nor'Wester,

> You will probably be surprised to learn that our A. McKenzie is determind [sic] to leave our Concern & the Country for ever. this has long been his determination, 'tho known only to a few—as he could not put it in execution till his Engagements with our House and the NWCo. were at an End. He has realized a handsome sum of Money & quits a very troublesome business—but at the present Juncture we could wish he still retaind [sic] his Situation as we cannot be too strong. . . . [16]

The existing terms of partnership in McTavish, Frobisher expired on November 30 of that year and would be the subject of renewal or revision at that time. Mackenzie was probably testing his worth to the firm by exerting pressure for promotion to senior-partner status. After all, what possible reason could he have for quitting the only occupation he knew and a business in which he had received promotions and profits? Early the next year McGillivray informs Cameron that

> Mr. A. McKenzie, after a great deal of havering and irresolution, at last determin'd on going to England without coming to any settlement with our House—his pretensions were unreasonable & inadmissible, & I believe finding at last he had carried matters too far—he would have preferr'd things were otherwise—tho' we parted not on the best of terms, nothing was past [sic] to prevent an amicable settlement, which we all wish for, & I sincerely hope when he has convers'd with men of more Experience and cooler Heads than his own, he will find it equaly [sic] desirable to terminate the matter amicably—& I have reason to think this is the Case—hard indeed would it be on all of us, *on me*

particularly, if after our long intimacy, we could only look on each other as Enemies in future . . . [17]

The second clue is an unsigned, undated item in Hudson's Bay Company Archives inscribed "Memorandum given Mr. Frobisher on new arrangement,"[18] and the handwriting is not unlike Mackenzie's. The memorandum contains proposals to reorganize McTavish, Frobisher under the joint managership of John Gregory, Alexander Mackenzie, and William McGillivray. Were these the pretensions that McGillivray speaks of as being "unreasonable and inadmissible" and that "had carried matters too far"? (Or is McGillivray referring to Mackenzie's reported attempts to get himself raised to copartner status or a rank senior to McGillivray?) Was Alexander Henry displaying his habitual shrewdness when he mentioned the impossibility of there being "two Caesars in Rome"? It is not difficult to imagine any of these ambitions alienating McGillivray's uncle. But the proposal—if Mackenzie's—of shutting McTavish out of the management of his own company must have roused all the fury latent in a proud, touchy, Highland temperament.

Until further records come to light, the only possible last word on the whole affair may have been said by John Fraser, McTavish's cousin and right-hand man in London. Shortly after Mackenzie's arrival there, he had a very frank exchange of views with Fraser, who summed things up in the written comment to McTavish that

McKenzie's abrupt departure from Montreal proceeds, I believe, entirely from a fit of ill humour, without any fixed plan or knowing himself what he would be at . . . as he has appeared to me all along to have been at his repentance for having quitted the concern, I told him that if he felt any regret or disappointment on that score, he must acknowledge it to be entirely his own act and deed; for after the repeated notice he had given you, he could not be surpris'd that you had taken your measures & could not listen to so late an application as he had made for continuing: to this he replied it was better you did not; for had matters then been settled, fresh differences would inevitably have immediately arisen . . . he has got an entire ascendant [ascendency] over your young men, and if driven to desperation, he may take steps ruinous to you. He has told myself your N[or]t[h] West business will be completely ruined; to others he has thrown out most violent threats of revenge, and I have had some hints too extravagant to mention.

He has been very modest on the score of money matters; before he asked me for a shilling, he deposited one of your bills of £500, which he has since begged to have to remit to Scotland; but he asks for nothing but for his subsistence, has, I'm convinced, no scheme of business in view, & does not think of interfering with you but by his influence with your people, which is the point you are to direct your whole attention to. . . .

P.S. It will be necessary to keep this communication private, as I have cause to think A. McK. is not uninformed of all that passes among you.[19]

Although Mackenzie failed to realize his ambitions under the auspices of McTavish, Frobisher, within two years he achieved a very different kind of success. In mid-December 1801 the *Voyages from Montreal* was published simultaneously in London and Edinburgh, a large, quarto volume of 550 pages illustrated by maps and containing an engraving of the author from the portrait by Sir Thomas Lawrence.

The book became a bestseller. Aided by generally favourable reviews and made popular by serialization in magazines, within two years of publication it had reappeared in several editions, including three in the United States. (The book was later translated into French, German, and Russian.) At a time in Britain's history when the conduct of her early military conflict with Napoleon Bonaparte* was uninspired and unsuccessful and

*One of Mackenzie's eventual readers is reported to have been Bonaparte himself. Apparently the Emperor of the French was toying with the idea of distracting British attention from Europe by attacking her North American possessions up the Mississippi and Ohio rivers and wanted detailed information on the Great Lakes region. One of Mackenzie's descendants claimed that she possessed a copy of the three-volume, French-language edition of the *Voyages* that was found in Napoleon's library at St. Helena after his death.

the British badly needed a hero, Alexander Mackenzie supplied a focus for hero-worship. Within fourteen months of the book's appearance, he was knighted by King George III and quickly became the favourite guest of every notable London hostess. On a visit to Scotland to see his two sisters, a great ball was organized for Mackenzie in the town of Ayr.

When the author of the *Voyages* remarks in the Preface that he "is not a candidate for literary fame," there is a deeper significance to his statement than the honest admission that his style of writing lacked distinction. He was offering the general reader a travel book in the form of an explorer's logbook—but he was also offering readers in high places an economic treatise on the fur trade and policies for a mighty expansion of it under the British flag. Mackenzie presents himself in the Preface as the hardbitten, tough-minded fur trader who not only contemplated the "practicability of penetrating across the continent of America" but was "animated by the desire to undertake the perilous enterprise." He encountered "perils by land and perils by water" and had "the passions and fears of others to control and subdue." But he was addressing a totally different audience when he crisply observed in the same Preface that

> Some account of the fur trade of Canada . . . of the native inhabitants, and of the extensive districts connected with it [the Northwest], forms a preliminary discourse, which will, I trust, prove interesting to a nation whose general policy is blended with, and whose prosperity is supported by the pursuits of commerce.

The preliminary discourse, entitled "A General History of the Fur Trade from Canada to the North-West", occupies approximately *one quarter* of the entire book.

The economic lesson is summed up in the book's concluding pages and is introduced in a polite, but pointed, manner.

> The following general, but short geographical view of the country [of northern North America] may not be improper to close this work, as well as some remarks on the

William McGillivray (1764-1825) was a lanky, good-looking, Highland Scot with hair as flamingly orange-red as his clan's tartan. The eldest of a family of six sons and six daughters, he immigrated to Montreal in 1784 to work for the fur firm operated by his uncle, Simon McTavish, who had financed the higher education of William and his brothers.

McGillivray spent nine years in various parts of the pays d'en haut as a Nor'Wester clerk. It was during his period of service on upper Churchill waters that he became friends with both Alexander Mackenzie and Roderic McKenzie. It was about the time that Mackenzie joined the Athabasca Department that he and McGillivray, in the latter's words, "took turns walking 6 and 700 miles on snow shoes for the pleasure of taking a Christmas dinner with a friend."

It has been observed that "a first-rate Indian trader is no ordinary man. He is a soldier-merchant and unites the gallantry of the one with the shrewdness of the other." McGillivray had both qualities in great measure, but particularly the latter. After the death of McTavish, his nephew took over the leadership of the individual fur concerns comprising the North West Company and managed their affairs ably and not a little ruthlessly. As Chief Superintendent of the Company he initiated and supported an era of expansion that is best remembered in the far-flung trading activities and bold explorations of Simon Fraser and David Thompson. However, this era ended tragically for McGillivray and many others when he decided to oppose Lord Selkirk's colonizing efforts in the Red River region. This decision also involved him in a contest with a tougher, more aggressive Hudson's Bay Company, which battled the Nor'Westers the length and breadth of the pays d'en haut, even as far north as Athabasca. The contest ruined the Nor'Westers financially, and they were forced to accept the absorption of themselves and their organization into the Hudson's Bay Company.

After the union of 1821, McGillivray was made a member of the London board that directed the entire Canadian fur trade, but he held this position for only four years. In the spring of 1825 he died of a rheumatic fever that had plagued him for years. Like Mackenzie, his life was probably shortened by the hardships of his time in the pays d'en haut.

Only two journals kept by McGillivray have survived. However, Marjorie Wilkin Campbell's book, McGillivray: Lord of the Northwest (Clarke, Irwin, 1962) is an absorbing recreation of his life and times.

Public Archives of Canada.

probable advantages that may be derived from advancing the trade of it under proper regulations, and by the spirit of commercial enterprise.

Anybody who reads this conclusion to the *Voyages* cannot but be impressed by Mackenzie's concise exposition of the major regions in North America north of the forty-fifth parallel. And he adds to this the logic of securing the trade of *all* those territories for Britain by "a commercial association" of the Hudson's Bay Company with "the merchants from Canada" who, despite the HBC charter, had "a right by prior possession as being successor to the subjects of France" and had been "the discoverers of a vast extent of country since added to His Majesty's territories, even to the Hyperborean and the Pacific Oceans." (Mackenzie thoughtfully sent a presentation copy of the *Voyages* to the Governor and Committee of the Hudson's Bay Company.) Then, he coolly adds that if the Hudson's Bay Company should decline to do so, there are "adventurers who would be willing, as they are able, to engage in and carry on the proposed commercial undertaking. . . . " He anticipated the necessity of persuading his trade colleagues, whether Nor'Westers or XY men, to join forces and form one huge transcontinental trading corporation under British auspices.

The essence of Mackenzie's reasoning is in the very last paragraphs of the *Voyages*, a clever, plausible argument but also a strangely prophetic vision of a British North America extending from sea to sea:

> . . . the Columbia* [River] is the line of communication from the Pacific Ocean . . . its banks . . . suitable to the residence of a civilized people . . . By opening up this intercourse between the Atlantic and Pacific Oceans and forming regular establishments through the interior and

---

*The route of the Columbia River was not known at this time. Mackenzie was mistakenly talking of the river he had been on—the Fraser—which he thought entered the Pacific at the Columbia's mouth (46° 20′N, 124°W), which was discovered in 1792 by Captain Robert Gray of the American merchantman *Columbia*. But Mackenzie's intuition was right: the Columbia was the navigable water route between the Rocky Mountains and the Pacific.

at both extremes as well as along the coasts and islands, the entire command of the fur trade of North America might be obtained . . . except that portion of it which the Russians have in the Pacific. To this may be added the fishing in both seas, and the markets of the four quarters of the globe. Such would be the field for commercial enterprise, and incalculable would be the produce of it, when supported by the operations of that credit and capital which Great Britain so pre-eminently possesses. Then would this country begin to be remunerated for the expenses it has sustained in discovering and surveying the coast of the Pacific Ocean, which is at present left to American adventurers, who, without regularity or capital . . . look altogether to the interest of the moment.

As the Canadian historian George M. Wrong has remarked, "The port of Vancouver and the Province of British Columbia are an answer to that prophecy."

Mackenzie was not content to enlist the sympathy of the general reader, who probably enjoyed an adventure story that reflected the hard-driving nature of its author and missed the economic pleas. In January 1802, barely a month after the publication of the *Voyages*, he submitted a detailed plan of imperial and commercial expansion to Lord Hobart, Secretary of State for War and the Colonies. Entitled "Preliminaries to the Establishment of a Permanent British Fishery and Trade in Furs &c. on the Continent and West Coast of North America," it is Mackenzie at his shrewdest and his most persuasive. The scope both of his thinking and his ambition is bold.

In the Preliminaries, Mackenzie sums up his views in the form of four points: the establishment of a "supreme" civil and military base at Nootka Sound on the west coast of Vancouver Island with subordinate stations at 46°N (the mouth of the Columbia) and 55° (at an unidentified location he calls Sea Otter Harbour); the repeal of the East India and South Sea Companies trade monopolies, or the requirement that they grant licences to British traders; the release by the Hudson's Bay Company of transit rights through all the "seas, Bays, Ports, Rivers, Lakes and Territories within the limits of its Charter"; the grant of these licences and rights to a London-based "Fishery and Fur Company" to exploit the Pacific fishing trade and the North American fur trade under the protection of the British government.

Mackenzie was proposing nothing less than the occupation of part of the North Pacific coast by the British government and a linkage of that coast with the St. Lawrence via a unified, regulated fur trade. His plan neatly conjoined imperial interest and private enterprise, which could hardly be expected to prosper without something of the special privileges given the Hudson's Bay, East India, and South Sea Companies. Mackenzie's solution was to establish yet another chartered company under the aegis of the British government. And since at this time the westernmost portion of the international boundary ran along the forty-ninth parallel technically as far as the Rocky Mountains, he was, in effect, nudging the British government to stake a claim to what are now the states of Washington and Oregon, if not also those of Montana and Idaho.

Over two years after leaving McTavish, Frobisher & Company, Mackenzie still must have been resentful of Simon McTavish. In the covering letter that accompanied his four proposals, there is a touch of acid in his advice to Lord Hobart that "some of the oldest members [of the North West Company] are likely to prefer continuing in the beaten track. Let such be at liberty to do as they please . . . I have not the slightest doubt of succeeding with all those whose *personal* [Mackenzie's italics] exertions are essential." However, he submitted an unbiased set of proposals, even to the point of observing in the notes accompanying the "Preliminaries" that " . . . the two Companies [North West and XY] already embarked in the fur trade from Montreal, including their several connections in London, must find their interests in coalescing. . . . " Lord Hobart suggested that the first step was to organize the union of all the Montreal fur interests, rather than just that of the old and new North West Companies, and Mackenzie left for Montreal in March of that year to attempt this. By proposing this initial move, Lord Hobart was able to gloss over the awkward facts that the government was not anxious to interfere with the vested rights of the Hudson's Bay, East

India, and South Sea Companies and did not have men and ships to spare to establish and maintain garrisons halfway round the world in the Pacific Northwest.

In October 1802 Mackenzie wrote from Montreal to Lord Hobart to report that he had not succeeded in bringing about a merging of fur interests. He had returned to find the trade plagued once more by the old evils of competition. Nor'Westers and XY men were at each other's throats—sometimes quite literally—and Mackenzie's time and energy had to be spent, as during his first years in the interior, in fighting for a share of the trade.

Mackenzie was not unaware of the steadily worsening conditions in the pays d'en haut. Although he had left Montreal in the fall of 1799, he had returned in the spring of 1800 to take part in the creation of a stronger XY Company by the inclusion of yet another fur company, Parker, Gerrard & Ogilvy (run by two Scots and an Irishman), which had also begun to contest the Nor'Westers. In 1801, this total association of interests became known as Alexander Mackenzie & Company and in 1802 as Sir Alexander Mackenzie & Company, although the more common reference to it was as the XY Company.

Just what part Mackenzie actually played in enlargening and strengthening the XY Company is not known. However, the XY copartners could hardly have carried on business as successfully as they did without a large measure of financial support from Mackenzie, whose name guaranteed virtually endless credit with certain London suppliers of trade goods. (Holding four of nineteen shares, Mackenzie became and remained the copartner with the largest investment in the Company.) And it is extremely unlikely that the XY group could have continued to challenge the Nor'Westers without Mackenzie's knowledge of the pays d'en haut—particularly Athabasca—and of the operational methods of the North West Company.

Even with Mackenzie's experienced advice, the contest was hardly waged on equal terms. Each organization was spending roughly similar amounts of money on goods and services, but the Nor'Westers had a decided edge in capital and

Canot, No. 25

2735

W. 19 Ballots de Marchandises, No.
G 5. 11. 12. 4. 18. 15. 7. 14. 8. 10.
F 33. 38. 10. 12. 35. 40. 11. 43. 15.

1 Ballots de Tabac noir,
- - - - de Tabac en carotes,
- - - - de N. W. Twist,
- - - - de Chaudières évasées,
- - - - de Chaudières de cuivre,
- - - - de Chaudières de fer blanc,
1 - - - - de Jambons,
- - - - de Bajoux,
Barils de Sel,
- - - de Graisse,
2 - - - de Poudre,
- - - de Sucre blanc,
- - - de Sucre brun,
4 - - - de Lard,
20 - - - de High Wines,
- - - de Rum,
- - - d'Esprit,
2 - - - de Bœuf,
2 - - - de Beurre,
2 - - - de Shrub,
1 - - - de Vin de Port,
- - - de Vin de Madère,
- - - de Vin rouge,
- - - d'Eau de vie de France,
- - - de Langues,
- - - de Saucisses,
- - - d'Orge,
- - - de Riz,
- - - de Fromage,
- - - de Raisins,
- - - de Figues,
- - - de Prunes,
2 Cassettes de Marchandifes, No. W 266, 255
2 Caisses de Fer, No. W 10. 21.
1 - - - - de Chapeaux, No. W 174.
- - - - de Couteaux, No.
- - - - de Fusils,
1 - - - - de Pièges, 153.
- - - - de Savon,
1 Maccarons de High Wines,
- - - - - - d'Esprit,
- - - - - - de Rum,
- - - - - - Mêlés,
Paquets de Fer,
- - - - d'Acier,
1 Sacs de Plomb,
1 - - - de Balles,
- - - de Pois,
- - - de Bled d'Inde d'1½ minot,
- - - ———— de 2 minots,
1 Corne

54 Pièces.

La Chine, [illegible] 1802

Les noms des hommes, savoir:

Amable Lavallée D
Jos. Le [illegible] G
Michel Ouellette D
Antoine Le [illegible]
Jos. [illegible] Lafontaine M
Jos. [illegible] M
J. B. [illegible] M
J. B. [illegible] M
[illegible] M

Vivres, savoir:

8 Sacs de Bifcuits,
2 - - - de Pois,
200 livres de Lard,

Les Agres, savoir:

1 Hache,
1 Plat de fer blanc,
1 Voile,
2 Prélats,
5 Lignes de Banc,
1 Chaudière,
1 Alêne,
1 rouleau d'Ecorce,
6 bottes de Wattap,
1 Crémaillière,
12 à 18 livres de Gomme.

A North West Company canoe bill of lading, which is dated 6 May, 1802, at Lachine, the depot a few miles west of Montreal from which brigades set off on the long route to Grand Portage.

Of a wide range of goods and supplies, this canot de maître carried 19 bales of merchandise, 1 of black tobacco, 1 of ham, 2 of gunpowder, 1 of pork fat, 20 of "high wine" (a potent mixture of rum and wine), 2 each of beef and butter, 2 of shrub (a mixture of orange or lemon juice, sugar, and rum or some other spirituous liquor), and 1 of port, together with hardware, hats, musket balls, and more high wine. As can be seen, the cargo totalled 64 pièces, each 90 pounds in weight. Note the considerable range of items that might be taken into the pays d'en haut. They ranged from sausages to soap, from types of tobacco and kettles (which were pot-like in shape and "nested" together without handles to conserve cargo space) to firearms, and were shipped in barrels, kegs, or cases.

In the upper right-hand column is a crew list. In the middle of the column are their sole provisions—salt biscuits, peas, and pork fat, which were mixed and boiled into a sort of paste guaranteed to stick to the eater's ribs. The remainder of the column itemizes the standard repair materials, notably wattape (spruce roots) and spruce gum for patching the canoe.

McCord Museum, Montreal.

in experienced personnel. According to Lord Selkirk,

> The only effectual competition that was ever carried
> on against the North West Company was that of the
> Company . . . established at Montreal under the appellation
> of the XY or New North West Company. . . . Though the
> New Company was powerfully supported with respect to
> capital and conducted by men of superior talents to most of
> those who managed the Old Company . . . they had to
> contend against every obstruction which their rivals could
> throw in their way. Among the obstacles, the Old North West
> Company not only engaged a larger number of men than
> they had ever [engaged] before, but also paid pensions to all
> the most active and experienced voyageurs who had already
> retired from service on condition that they should not enter
> into the employment of their rivals. From these causes, the
> New Company were always much inferior in numbers at
> their wintering posts in the Indian country, and the
> disproportion was perhaps never less than as two to one.[20]

Of course, the Nor-Westers were old hands at securing maximum returns. They knew how to cajole or bully Indians into bringing them furs pledged to rival traders. They knew the weakness of one trapper for gaudy sashes and the craving of another for tobacco or liquor. The wintering partners were also ordered to keep close watch on XY traders during the spring, when Indians made their final hunt. Few prime pelts were available at this season since it was the time of year when hibernating animals were emaciated and their pelts almost moth-eaten in appearance. But all was grist to the Nor'Wester mill.

Naturally, the XY winterers received similar instructions. They were urged not to rely solely on barter at their posts but to send out their clerks among Indian groups, checking on Nor'Wester activities and shadowing them wherever they went. Even Alexander Henry the Younger (nephew of the Alexander Henry who was a contemporary of Peter Pond and the Frobishers), an experienced winterer, records of this period that on one occasion when he found it necessary to visit a particular band of Indians, he was forced to set off at midnight on a dark, rainy night "to escape the XY who was on the watch."

All this cloak-and-dagger activity meant increased costs because more men, goods, and trading posts were required. It also bred violence. Scuffles and fist fights were common; canoes were hijacked and their cargoes taken over or destroyed. There was even killing in the pays d'en haut early in 1802. Joseph Maurice Lamothe, an XY clerk, had collected some furs owed by Indians and had piled them inside a tipi he was using for an overnight stop on his way back to his post. James King of the North West Company, out on a similar mission for his employers, was disappointed and angered by the poor-quality pelts he had secured and tried to steal the furs in Lamothe's tipi. Lamothe shot him, and King bled to death.

When word of the incident reached Montreal, it must have stirred official memories of earlier deaths, those of Jean-Etienne Waden and John Ross, memories that were kept alive during Lamothe's appearance before a grand jury in Montreal late in 1802. Mackenzie, who was never at any time in his career a violent man, was subject to the same unpleasant recollections. Writing in 1802 to Lord Hobart, the Colonial Secretary, on a different matter, he nonetheless felt compelled to insert the remark that

> I cannot too strongly entreat his Lordship's attention to the propriety and necessity of establishing as speedily as possible such a jurisdiction as shall prevent the contending fur companies from abusing any power which superiority of strength or numbers may accidentally confer. . . .

A curb on lawlessness was not long in coming. The very next year, Parliament passed the Canada Jurisdiction Act "extending the Jurisdiction of the Courts of Lower and Upper Canada [Quebec and Ontario] to the Trial and Punishment of Persons guilty of Crimes and Offences within certain parts of North America adjoining to the said Provinces." While the Act made little or no difference to the conduct of the trade in the pays d'en haut at this time, it was clear warning to traders to reform their methods and seek a common interest.

However, the .worst feature of the struggle was the prodigality with which each company lavished bribes of liquor on its customers. Exploitation and corruption of Indians was conducted on a scale never seen before. At the height of the struggle, the XY Company was using an average of 5,000 gallons of spirits a year. But the Nor'Westers, with the advantage of freight boats on the Great Lakes as well as canoe brigades, were employing at least 15,000 gallons annually in their trading operations. The significance of 20,000 gallons of spirits being handed out in the period 1802-04 is that, in the years immediately prior to 1802, the North West Company averaged about 9,000 gallons annually.

Liquor flowed like water in the pays d'en haut. Traders' journals casually record many commonplace incidents of mayhem and murder caused by a highly concentrated form of alcohol known in the trade as "high wine" and usually composed of two parts of wine to one of rum or brandy. A historian of the fur trade has written a particularly graphic account of the brutally cynical manner in which the wintering partners of each company plied their customers with liquor

> . . . to get them to come to the post, to welcome them on arrival, to buy their loyalty, to keep it, to induce them to default on the credit they had had from the opposition, to put them in a mood for trade, to inflate the price of goods, to reward them for virtue, to express your everlasting admiration of their brave deeds, or because they drove you crazy begging for it.
>
> They were not lovable when in liquor and they loved neither one another nor anyone else . . . Cautoquince bites Terre Grasse's nose off; a relative finds it in the straw and bandages it on again. Wayquetoe shoots an arrow through his wife and with another wings a gallant who may have been eyeing her . . . A four-year-old child has his buttocks shot off while papa is high. A squaw leaves her husband's lodge—a legal divorce—but presently, getting drunk, the old husband and the new one quarrel over the custody of her baby. Each grabbing it by a leg, "they began to pull and haul; on a sudden the father gave a jerk and, the other resisting, the child was torn asunder."[21]

Debauching the western tribes as a matter of basic policy was at its worst between 1802 and 1804 and might have gone on for several years had it not been for the sudden illness and death of Simon McTavish early in July, 1804. With the "old lion of Montreal" gone, the cooler wisdom of his successor, McGillivray, prevailed.

Although McTavish had convened and actually attended a special meeting of the winterers at Grand Portage in July 1802,* in the course of which the Company was reorganized on a ninety-two share basis and stringent economies written into this agreement, there had been no thought in his mind of seeking a union of the old and the new North West companies. McTavish had dominated the Montreal business scene too long and too successfully to entertain any idea of a merger like that of 1787 with Gregory, McLeod, or even the easy solution of 1792 when he had bought off Todd, McGill and Forsyth, Richardson with a few North West Company shares. As expansion-minded as ever, McTavish diversified Company interests by negotiating the rental from the British government of the St. Lawrence fisheries at what were called the King's Posts and saw to it that new fishing posts were established on various lakes in what is now northern Quebec. And shortly after Mackenzie took charge of the XY group, McTavish ordered a further expansion of the trade, this time by openly defying the Hudson's Bay Company charter. He sent one expedition overland from the St. Lawrence valley to establish a trade outlet on Moose River and the other by ship into the Bay itself to establish a depot on Charleton Island. The Hudson's Bay Company had refused polite offers in the past to sell him transit rights through Hudson Bay. Perhaps a mixture of force and argument would change the Company's mind, the more so since Mackenzie had his eye firmly fixed on the Bay route to and from the pays d'en haut. Like his rival, McTavish saw that the Montreal organization that gained the use of the Bay as a transport route would have far easier access to Athabasca and

*This was the last meeting ever held there. The American government had given the Nor'Westers notice to quit Grand Portage, and they were already building Fort William, a new, larger depot forty-five miles farther east along the north shore of Superior at the mouth of the Kaministiquia River, which flows through modern Thunder Bay, Ontario.

would also be able to expand its operations into fur regions that lay beyond the Rocky Mountains.

McGillivray took a different view. At the partners' summer meeting at Grand Portage in 1803, he noted that while the latest gross profits—just short of £200,000—were the largest in the Company's history, five very costly years of opposition had steadily reduced net returns and necessitated the introduction of still further economics. He was particularly worried about the flagrant invasion of the Bay. The two-pronged attack had taken thousands of pounds to organize, with no prospect of any immediate return in furs. And McGillivray feared that any law proceedings brought by an infuriated Hudson's Bay Company would result in the Nor'Westers having to pay as much money again in court costs and damages. In addition, there had been rumours of "regulations of control" of the trade by British officials shocked at the killing of John King and angered by accounts of drunken, demoralized Indians. Thus, after the news of his uncle's death reached him at Fort William late in July, 1804, McGillivray was back in Montreal the next month. By October he had negotiated terms of union with Sir Alexander Mackenzie & Company "to put an end to opposition and to avoid the waste of property attending thereon and to carry on the trade in a more advantageous manner. . . . "

McGillivray's opponents, too, were worried enough by years of expensive competition and the thought of government control to welcome a coalition. From Mackenzie's point of view, it was 1787 all over again, when Gregory, McLeod had merged with the North West Company. If you can't beat your enemies, you do the next best thing: you join them. However, although Mackenzie was allowed back into Nor'Wester ranks, his defection had not been forgotten, and it was not going to be forgiven.

The amalgamation proved to be another setback in Mackenzie's career. In 1802 he had been unsuccessful in imposing the logic of his views upon the British government or the rival companies. In 1804, he was effectively shut out of the Montreal fur trade. The further reorganization of the North West Company in November of that year expanded the number of shares to one hundred, but the division of them was on a three-to-one basis: seventy-five to the Nor'Westers and twenty-five to their former rivals. Control remained in the hands of McTavish, Frobisher, and Mackenzie was denied any role in management. The result was summed up by that veteran fur merchant, Isaac Todd, in a letter to an acquaintance.

> There is a coalition of the two North West Companies which will be to their interest and comfort and be useful to the society here. As far as my influence went with Mr. McGillivray I promoted it. The new [North West] Company is to have one-fourth of the whole but the business to be conducted by the old, and Sir Alexander Mackenzie is excluded from any interference. With him and McGillivray there will, I fear, never be intimacy.[22]

As W. Stewart Wallace, an eminent chronicler of the trade has observed, in Mackenzie's exclusion "there was to be seen, without doubt, the dead hand of Simon McTavish."

Mackenzie did what little he could in the circumstances. Four days after signing alongside the Nor'Westers, he and his colleagues also signed articles of agreement to continue the separate legal existence of Sir Alexander Mackenzie & Company. This gave all of them a financial stake for the future: in addition to their portion of profits from the North West Company, Mackenzie and his associates would also receive profits gained by his organization through supplying goods and services (warehousing, transport, etc.) required by the North West Company and from the sale of one fourth of all furs it exported.

After the amalgamation, the North West Company under McGillivray's leadership went on to compete with an aroused and more active Hudson's Bay Company and to expand the fur trade. Simon Fraser followed Mackenzie's old route up the Peace and Parsnip Rivers into what is now central British Columbia and established the Company's New Caledonia Department. Fraser's friend and fellow wintering partner, David Thompson, found two passes through the Rocky Mountains and built up the Columbia Department. Ultimately, in 1811, Thompson found the navigable canoe route to and from the

Roderic McKenzie (d. 1844) never liked the crude commercialism of the fur trade. A gentle, introspective man and something of a bookworm, he preferred to spend his time as a clerk reading the classics. He also attempted to become an author. While in charge of Fort Chipewyan, McKenzie began compiling an anthropological account of all of the Indian groups in the Athabasca region with the intention of working out an analogy of their customs with those of European and Asian races. He collected an enormous mass of material but got no further than the first chapter of the book he proposed to write. (This chapter, written up in a huge, ledger-like volume, is preserved today in the Public Archives of Canada, Ottawa.)

McKenzie grew to loathe the trade so much that, despite being made a partner in McTavish, Frobisher & Co. in 1800 and a Nor'Wester agent the same year, in 1801 he sold his shares in the North West Company. He remained a dormant partner in McTavish, Frobisher (later McTavish, McGillivrays & Co.) until the firm's failure in 1825.

McKenzie spent twenty-one years in politics as a member of the Legislative Council of Lower Canada. He also devoted many years to gathering various notes, letters, documents, and manuscripts with which to compile a history of the fur trade in the Northwest, but he neither published these materials nor arranged them for publication.

In 1856 Louis F. R. Masson, who became a prominent Quebec lawyer and politician, married one of McKenzie's granddaughters, and partly through her became interested in these materials. Masson acquired, edited, and eventually published many of them in his Les Bourgeois de la Compagnie du Nord-Ouest *(2 vols., Quebec, 1889-90), which includes a section entitled "Reminiscences by the Honorable Roderick McKenzie, being chiefly a synopsis of letters from Sir Alexander Mackenzie." This contains interesting source material on the trade and various Nor'Wester contemporaries of Alexander and Roderic. However, the reproduction in the "Reminiscences" of the former's letters should be regarded with considerable caution. Masson, like many editors of his day and age, amended and abridged them to suit himself. The reader is advised to consult Kaye Lamb's* The Journals and Letters of Sir Alexander Mackenzie *(Cambridge University Press, 1971) for a much more faithful version of the explorer's correspondence.*

Pacific that Mackenzie (and Fraser) had failed to find—the Columbia River. Its discovery was to give the Company a further ten years of life.

All of these activities and successes must have brought Mackenzie pleasure and pain. His explorations had been fully justified, yet he had had absolutely no hand in directing their fulfilment. Nor did he accomplish anything of note after being barred from the management of the North West Company. At first he devoted himself to politics. Elected in August 1804 to the legislature of Lower Canada (Quebec) as the member for Huntingdon County, he quickly became bored. By January 1805 he was writing from Quebec City to Roderic (in "Dear Sir" terms) that "I am heartily tired of legislation. I sincerely wish that those who thought themselves my friends in being the means of getting me so honourable a situation had been otherwise employed." He found the society of his fellow politicians very agreeable, although he noted that the "attentions I universally receive" were more often from strangers than people with whom he was even slightly acquainted. He was a fish out of water.

It probably came as no great surprise to Roderic when in November 1805 he received another "Dear Sir" letter, a rather pathetic one this time, written aboard the *Pallas*, a Royal Navy frigate departing for England.

> Although I have not anything worth troubling you with, I cannot let slip this last opportunity that offers of addressing you on this side of the Atlantic. . . . Never mind the folly of the times; for my own part I am determined to make myself as comfortable as circumstances will allow. I have a large field before me. I do not leave Canada without regret. . . .

Despite his brave reassurance to Roderic that he had a large field before him, Mackenzie overestimated his ability to make any mark on it. In 1808 he again attempted to secure a trade charter from the British government. Introducing himself this time as a partner in the North West Company, he requested a charter for the Nor'Westers that would give them the same rights on the Pacific that the Hudson's Bay Company enjoyed in the interior of the continent. His arguments were impressive. In 1803, the United States had bought France's remaining holdings in North America, and the Louisiana Purchase as it was called had added to the States a vast region stretching from the Mississippi to the Rocky Mountains. Two years later, President Thomas Jefferson had sent the Lewis and Clark expedition to stake an early American claim to sovereignty of the Pacific Coast.* Thus the lands and trade of the Columbia basin could fall into American hands. But Mackenzie's application was passed from department to department, and the British cabinet was too engrossed in fighting Napoleon Bonaparte to spare any time to debate a trade and colonization scheme halfway around the world. Nothing ever came of the proposal.

Because he had good reason to distrust the slow progress of government towards a point of ultimate action, in 1808 Mackenzie began to buy Hudson's Bay Company stock, which had sunk from £100 to £60 a share, thanks to the aggressive trading practices of the Nor'Westers. His object was to purchase control of the Company's operations and secure at least Hudson Bay transit rights for the Nor'Westers, if not also exclusive trading rights in Athabasca. He had already tried to buy the Company outright. While a director of the XY group, Mackenzie had ordered its London agents, Phyn, Ellice, & Co., to make an offer to purchase. Edward Ellice, a senior partner, offered £103,000, but was refused. According to Ellice, the transaction failed only because "part of the stock was found to be the property of infants, and other persons incapable of giving title." Perhaps this was the reason, perhaps not. Apart from its considerable assets in forts, goods, and ships, and an annual gross in furs of about £30,000, the Hudson's Bay Company had some £40,000 invested in stocks and bonds. Why would the Company accept an offer that was not overly generous?

Ironically, Mackenzie was aided this time in his objective by another, much wealthier Scot, Thomas Douglas, fifth Earl of Selkirk, who had his own reasons for seeking power to manage H. B. C. policy. Lord Selkirk's interest was, in his own words, "at the western extremity of Canada, upon the Waters

*President Jefferson had bought a copy of an 1803 American edition of the *Voyages* and found himself in complete agreement with Mackenzie's ideas on transcontinental dominion, hence the Lewis-and-Clark expedition.

which fall into Lake Winnipeck [sic]," where, "with a moderate exertion of industry" colonists could be sure of a "comfortable subsistence." He dreamed of founding a settlement at Red River. (It is not clear why Selkirk chose this area, but he may have got the idea from reading Mackenzie's *Voyages*, where there is a favourable description of the Red River region in the "General History", or simply from chatting with Mackenzie himself.)

By 1810 Mackenzie, Selkirk, and a group of associates had invested several thousand pounds in H. B. C. stock. But by this time the former had discovered his ally's motive—the establishment of a settlement in the Nor'Westers' Red River Department—and Mackenzie ended up opposing Selkirk's plan. With his usual astuteness, Mackenzie sensed trouble: if farming spread all over a region where buffalo, the source of huge Nor'Wester supplies of pemmican, were accustomed to roam freely, the great herds would abandon the Red River region. This could create immense difficulties, if not hardship, for men serving in the pays d'en haut.

By February, 1811, Selkirk had not only persuaded the Governor and Committee of the Hudson's Bay Company to accept his colonization scheme but had gained total personal control of it. Thereupon, Mackenzie, as a shareholder, sought to delay matters by insisting—as he had a right to—that Selkirk's project be examined and approved by a General Court of the Company, that is, by a general meeting of all shareholders. This manoeuvre also gave Mackenzie a breathing space in which to try and purchase enough further shares to sway a decision against Selkirk at the General Court. But few shares became available, and time ran out on Mackenzie. In the course of the general meeting, Selkirk was able to persuade the shareholders to accept the colonization venture, and the Red River colony was, in effect, born on that last day of May, 1811.

Mackenzie could do little thereafter but harass Selkirk's lieutenants in various minor ways as they organized the dispatch of the first group of settlers. A bitter, ruinously expensive struggle developed between Selkirk and the Nor'Westers, a struggle in which Mackenzie played no active part. That contest took place in the pays d'en haut and, ultimately, in the law courts of

Upper and Lower Canada. But the genesis of the whole affair was yet another failure on Mackenzie's part to get control of the Hudson's Bay Company and, through it, unify the fur trade.

In 1812, at the age of forty-eight, Mackenzie married Geddes Mackenzie, the daughter of a Scots merchant resident in London. The Reverend D. Masson, an Edinburgh clergyman who knew her during her many years of widowhood, described her as "one of the most beautiful women I ever saw." She was not related by blood to Sir Alexander, although her forbears came from a part of mainland Scotland quite close to her husband's boyhood home in the Hebrides.

Geddes' paternal grandfather had purchased Avoch, an estate on a peninsula of land in northern Scotland bordering the Moray Firth and had willed it to her and her sister Margaret. About the time of the marriage, Sir Alexander purchased Avoch, which was situated on a peninsula of land known locally as the Black Isle. He and his wife spent only part of each year there because they also maintained a Mayfair town house and enjoyed the giddy social whirl maintained by London's upper crust of gentry and nobility.

In the years following 1812 Sir Alexander's involvement in fur-trade matters was little more than that of a consultant. He was still a partner in the North West Company, and Edward ("Bear") Ellice, a fellow partner and London businessman, often sought his comments and advice on a gradual revival of competition and violence in the pays d'en haut. The Nor'Westers were now battling an aroused Selkirk and his followers and also traders from the Bay, who were moving well inland and even setting up shop in the Athabasca country. But with William McGillivray now travelling to London to transact Company business and even submitting his proposals to the government for expansion of the trade, there was less and less for Mackenzie to do. In any case, he had had his fill of knocking on official doors and getting nowhere. In May, 1811, he helped draw up a petition, addressed to King George III, requesting that, in particular, the North West Company be given exclusive trading privileges between the Rocky Mountains and the Pacific. But the request was not allowed by His Majesty's legal advisors. A similar appeal in June 1812 to a government trade committee was unsuccessful. And yet another like petition in 1812, this time addressed to a cabinet minister, was refused.

Perhaps it was a fortunate circumstance that Mackenzie and his wife thoroughly enjoyed the busy London social season and a connection with Court circles through Edward, Duke of Kent, one of King George III's sons. (In one of his letters to Sir Alexander, the Duke mentions that his wife was "getting over the effects of weaning her Infant." At a later date, the infant became Queen Victoria.) In the summer, members of London society retired to their country homes to recuperate and prepare themselves for the endless dinners, parties, and balls of the next social season. At this time of year Sir Alexander and Lady Mackenzie journeyed north to Avoch, where, as befitted a laird, he took a keen interest in the life of the district. He himself initiated several local improvements, which included establishing oyster beds in a nearby bay and the construction of a sea wall to protect the road between the village of Avoch and the local burgh of Fortrose. And by 1819 Mackenzie also had a family of two infant sons and a daughter to occupy part of his attention.

Early in 1819 Mackenzie renewed correspondence with Roderic (now addressed as "My Dear Sir") after personally allowing contact to lapse for almost two years. In the letter he mentions learning about Selkirk's struggle with the Nor'Westers from the newspapers and goes on to remark with great shrewdness that he would not be surprised to see a serious change take place in the direction of the North West Company's affairs. He adds, "To me this can be of no consequence, as I think it would be unjust, as well as impolitic, to continue me or any other person upon the establishment as a dormant partner. I shall be most happy, however, to see the business continued and carried on with vigor. . . . " After enquiring kindly after the health of his cousin's youngsters, particularly the boy who had been given the name of Alexander, and assuring Roderic of the good health of his own children, Mackenzie goes on,

. . . I have been overtaken with the consequences of my sufferings in the North West. I think it is of the same nature with Mr. McGillivray's complaint, but it has not yet arrived at a serious crisis. I have, in obedience to orders, become a water drinker and milk sop. I have not tasted wine, spirituous or malt liquor for several months, which I think has been of service to me.

The symptoms of the disorder are very disagreeable and most uncomfortable. The exercise of walking, particularly if uphill, brings on a headache, stupor or dead pain, which at once pervades the whole frame, attended with a listlessness and apathy which I cannot well describe. Exercise in a carriage, if not violent, has a beneficial effect. The great Doctor Hamilton of Edinburgh calls it a shake of the constitution and I am acting now under his guidance. . . .

Lady Mackenzie is sitting by me, and the children are playing on the floor. The former joins me most cordially in kind regards to you, Mrs. McKenzie, and your young family.

Yours truly and sincerely,

Alex. Mackenzie

Now fifty-five, he had just about a year to live. His "disorder" seems to have been Bright's disease, a term applied to various forms of bacterial infection, and gradual degeneration, of the kidneys. It was probably caused, or at the very least aggravated, by the primitive conditions he had endured for so many years in the pays d'en haut. (In the course of returning from the Pacific he casually noted a swelling of the ankles that made walking very difficult and very painful; this edema or dropsical condition is one symptom of Bright's disease.) Dieting and rest prolonged his life into 1820, but in May of that year Roderic received a letter from a Mr. Kenneth Dowie.

Dear Sir,

It is with the greatest regret I have to inform you of the death of my uncle Sir Alexander Mackenzie.

Accompanied by Lady Mackenzie and children, he was on his way from Edinburgh to [Avoch] Rosshire and was suddenly taken ill at Mulnain, near Dunkeld, on the 11th of March and expired the following morning.

171

Epilogue

Barely twelve months after Mackenzie's body was laid to rest in the graveyard of the little church at Avoch, the British government was induced, principally by the lobbying of Montreal and London fur merchants, to arrange a merger of the North West Company and the Hudson's Bay Company under the name of the latter, and grant it a monopoly of trade throughout the entire western interior and on the Pacific coast. This union, formally signed on March 26, 1821, vindicated the logic of Mackenzie's commercial views. Unable to overcome the Hudson's Bay Company's great advantage of cheaper, direct access to the pays d'en haut and thus to the Pacific, the Nor'Westers were forced by years of steadily rising costs to accept terms of union with the Bay organization.

As for Mackenzie's political reasons for a unified, expanded fur trade, under the leadership of another Scot, George Simpson, this new, stronger Hudson's Bay Company went on to challenge the Russians and the Americans on the Pacific coast and succeeded in establishing a British claim to a large part of the coastal Northwest. This claim had far-reaching consequences. In 1846, when the British and American governments negotiated a settlement of the boundary beyond the Rocky Mountains, the United States secured what was known as the Oregon Territory, but Great Britain retained those regions immediately north of the 49th parallel that later became known as British Columbia. Without an outlet on the Pacific, it is extremely doubtful if there would ever have been a Canada. Without access to the Pacific, Canada would probably have been unable to resist absorption into the United States.

An eminent scholar and historian of exploration in North America says of Mackenzie,

Well in advance of anyone else he determined the commercial axis of the continent and he foresaw the exact shape of the last imperial struggle that was implicit in

172

continentalism. In courage, in the faculty of command, in ability to meet the unforeseen with resources of craft and skill, in the will that cannot be overborne, he has had no superior in the history of American exploration. But he is a hard man to like. The Scots who were nine-tenths of the North West Company's aristocracy average remarkably high in arrogance, caste brutality, and the paralysis of personal emotions that is called reserve. Mackenzie had them in a measure that raised him above the rest.[23]

It is an unflattering but not unfitting epitaph.

Appendix of Indian Groups

ASSINIBOINE

A Siouan-speaking people related to the Dakota or Sioux family of plains Indians, the Assiniboine migrated at some time or other from the central plains of the continent to the Lake of the Woods region. Then, in the eighteenth century, they relocated in districts south and west of Lake Winnipeg, notably the broad valley of the Assiniboine River. Their name, an Ojibwa word meaning "the people that cook with hot stones," probably stems from their one-time habit of gathering and boiling great quantities of the wild rice growing in the Lake of the Woods-Rainy Lake region. Mackenzie refers to them as the "Stone-Indians or Assiniboins," the former term being a common one in fur traders' journals.

In the eighteenth century, the Assiniboine were mainly buffalo hunters, although they often trapped fur-bearing animals and used their pelts for trading purposes with other Indians and also with the French and the British. A fierce, aggressive people, the Assiniboine warred off and on with their kin, the Sioux, and fought with their neighbours to the west, the Blackfoot, for control of what are now the Canadian prairies.

BEAVER, DOGRIB, HARE, SEKANI, SLAVE,
YELLOWKNIFE

The fact that Pond, Mackenzie, and other Nor'Westers in the Athabasca Department had no difficulty communicating with the various tribal groups in the Northwest is not as remarkable as might appear. All these Indians belonged to a common linguistic stock, the huge Athapaskan-speaking family. (These natives used the term Déné, "people," to describe themselves.) They are often described as the "babiche people". Of all Indians, the Athapaskans—which include the Chipewyan—are most given to the use of *babiche*, strips of tanned caribou or deerskin used for lacing snowshoes, making nets, bags, snares, and bindings of various kinds.

Most of the Athapaskans were—and still are—

nomadic, occupying the northern reaches of the vast trans-continental northern or boreal forest that stretches from south of Hudson Bay all the way north and west into Arctic regions. They made a precarious living by hunting, fishing, and trapping. Essentially caribou hunters and inured to the long, severe, northern winter, they had a simple culture that reflected only an eternal need to find enough food to survive a harsh environment—spears, bows and arrows, stone or flint arrowheads and knives, snowshoes, toboggans, birchbark canoes, skin and bark containers, deer or fur clothing. It took anywhere from eight to ten caribou skins to provide a man with a shirt, leggings, robe, moccasins, cap, and mittens; and almost as many to equip him with a plentiful supply of babiche.

The Beaver occupied much of the valley of the Peace River, the original Indian name for which was Tsades, "River of Beavers."

The Dogrib, so-called because of their legendary descent from a dog, roamed west of the Mackenzie approximately midway between Great Slave and Great Bear lakes and were an edge-of-the-woods people, spending almost as much time hunting on the Arctic barrens as in the boreal forest.

The Hare, as timid as the animal that provided much of their sustenance and also their name, lived farther down the Mackenzie on either side of the river.

The Sekani, the "People of the Rocks" (i.e., of the Rocky Mountains), occupied the basins of the Parsnip and Finlay Rivers and the upper waters of the Peace. Harassed by both Beaver and Cree, some of the Sekani eventually moved westward into what is now central British Columbia.

According to Mackenzie, the Slave were neighbours of the Beaver, inhabiting the fringes of Lake Athabasca, the Slave River, and the western half of Great Slave Lake, although the Cree seem to have driven them farther down the Mackenzie. In general a mild, peaceable people, the Slave—a Cree term of contempt—were actually feared by neighbouring bands, who considered them very adept at witchcraft.

The Yellowknife, or Copper, Indians—whom Mackenzie identifies as "Red-Knife" Indians—hunted the land northeast of Great Slave and Great Bear lakes and, like the Chipewyan, were an edge-of-the-woods people who often spent summers pursuing caribou and muskoxen on the barren grounds. All three names, of course, refer to their use of copper instead of stone or bone.

BELLA BELLA, BELLA COOLA, SHUSHWAP

These tribes were members of the Salishan linguistic stock, a group of Indians who seem to have belonged originally to the great Algonkian-speaking family of tribes of central and eastern North America but who settled in what is now the northwest United States and British Columbia. The coast-dwelling Bella Bella and Bella Coola were linguistically related but formed distinctly separate cultural groups. As indicated in the narrative, the Shushwap preferred to live along the upper waters of the Fraser River. The meaning of each of these three tribal names is unknown.

Salish Indians lived in a region of heavily forested mountains, tumbling streams and rivers, misty valleys and canyons, and, on the coast, alongside the often fog-shrouded waters of coastal inlets. Their principal occupation was fishing for salmon, halibut and cod. These natives lived in small, semi-permanent fishing settlements, each usually forming an autonomous unit led by a headman picked for his achievements, ability, or wisdom. Salmon—netted, speared, or trapped in rivers—was the principal food supply, supplemented by roots and berries of several kinds and small game. When their food reserves of smoked salmon ran low and other sources were scarce, the Salish gathered mosses and the inner bark of certain trees and cooked these into an unappetizing but sustaining gruel.

The Salish practised neither agriculture nor pottery making but were highly skilled in making beautifully designed and woven grass baskets and mats. They were also skilled in using dog and goat hair mixed with cedar bark to make blankets decorated with simple geometric patterns.

BLACKFOOT, GROS VENTRE, SARSI

Mackenzie never encountered one of the strongest and most aggressive Indian nations of the eighteenth century, the Blackfoot or Blackfeet, whose territory stretched several hundred miles east from the Alberta and Montana foothills of the Rocky Mountains and extended from the North Saskatchewan River almost as far south as the upper waters of the Missouri. However, he made many enquiries about them and estimated their warrior population to be about twenty-five hundred in the year 1800, which suggests a total of about nine to ten thousand persons.

A confederacy of Piegan, Blood, and the Blackfoot proper, and often referred to collectively as the Blackfoot or Blackfeet, they were an Algonkian-speaking group composed of independent tribal units joined loosely by a tradition of common origin, a common language, common customs, and frequent intermarriage. Under their protection were two smaller groups: the Gros Ventre ("Big Belly"), or Atsina* as the Blackfoot called them, and, strangely, the Sarsi or Sarcee of the Athapaskan-speaking family, who had drifted south from their original home in the valley of the Peace River. Like their enemies the Assiniboine, the Blackfoot followed the Plains Indian way of life—the buffalo hunt, which provided them with food, clothing, and their conical hide tents or tipis. The name Blackfoot refers to their moccasins, either because these were painted black or were scorched by the ashes of prairie grass fires.

Sometime in the middle or late eighteenth century the Blackfoot became middlemen in the fur trade, exchanging HBC and Nor'Wester goods for pelts obtained by mountain

---

*Some authorities state that the name Gros Ventre is from their location near the Big Belly River, one of the tributaries of the South Saskatchewan. A likelier explanation is a European misunderstanding of the Indian sign-language term for "beggar". The sign, a moving of a hand out in front of the body to indicate a large, fat, belly, means "one who always wants more to eat and is never satisfied." The name Atsina has much the same meaning.

tribes in the west, who were intimidated by regular raids and frequent pillage.

The Blackfoot confederacy was a warrior society composed of various grades of military-like rank ranging from young initiates to the oldest and most experienced men. As a people they were famed for their ferocity, close sense of kinship, a ribald and often mocking sense of humour, and a well-developed ability to steal horses from other Indians.

CARRIER

On his journeys to and from the Pacific Coast via what he named the West Road River, Mackenzie and his men encountered the Carrier, so called from their curious custom of compelling widows to carry on their backs for some years the charred bones of their husbands. These Indians occupied much of the lake and river country of what is now central British Columbia.

Unlike the other native groups of the Pacific coast, the Carrier were members of the huge Athapaskan-speaking group of Indians. However, like neighbouring groups, they were heavily dependent upon fish, notably the salmon, as a food staple, supplemented by edible roots and berries. And, like the coastal tribes, the Carrier observed the custom of the potlatch. Every important event from the construction of a large house to a successful war raid resulted in a feast and the distribution of gifts.

CHIPEWYAN

Mackenzie describes them as sober, timorous, vagrant, and the most peaceful Indians known in North America, although, before their great enemies the Cree acquired firearms, the Chipewyan did have a record as an aggressive people. He identifies them as being of the "Dene" stock, meaning that they were members of the great Athapaskan-speaking family of Indians found in the forests and barren lands of the Northwest. Until Mackenzie's time, they were the most numerous Athapaskan group in northern Canada and occupied an area extending west from Hudson Bay and north of the Churchill River to the eastern fringes of Lake Athabasca and Great Bear Lake. The great smallpox epidemic of 1780/81 destroyed the majority of the Chipewyan.

According to Samuel Hearne of the Hudson's Bay Company, it killed nine-tenths of them.

The Chipewyan were really an edge-of-the-woods people, living in small bands and ekeing out a primitive existence by hunting caribou in the forests and on the Arctic barrens, by snaring game, and by fishing. For many years they acted as middlemen between the HBC and the tribes of the Mackenzie delta. Their name is supposedly derived from a Cree term meaning "pointed skins," a contemptuous reference to the form in which the Chipewyan dried their beaver skins. Some authorities, however, claim that it refers to the shape of the Chipewyans' shirts, which came to a point at the front and back and were ornamented with tails.

CREE

An Algonkian-speaking group, the Cree are frequently mentioned by Mackenzie and rather surprisingly he characterizes them as a mild, affable people. He also remarks that "of all the natives which I have seen on this continent, the Knisteneaux women are the most comely. Their figure is generally well proportioned. . . . their complexion has less of that dark tinge which is common to these savages who have less cleanly habits."

The name "Cree" developed from "Cris," a shortened form of the French term Kristenaux or Kristeneaux, although Mackenzie consistently spells the name Knisteneaux.

Of course, Mackenzie encountered the "affable" Cree after they had been greatly reduced in numbers and influence by the widespread smallpox epidemic of 1780/81. Prior to that time, they were a fierce, highly competitive people who moved north and west in search of furs from their original homeland of forest and lake immediately south of Hudson Bay. Ultimately, the Cree controlled an immense territory corresponding in size to today's northern Manitoba, Saskatchewan, and Alberta. Armed with HBC and Nor'Wester firearms, they even raided up the Peace River into the Rockies and all the way down into the Mackenzie delta, often displacing the Chipewyan as middlemen between the HBC (and, later, the Nor'Westers) and northern Indians. Indeed the Chipewyan, the largest and strongest of the Athapaskan-speaking peoples, were invaded and, in effect, subjugated by the Woodland or Swampy Cree. Another branch, the Plains Cree, expanded onto the prairies and quickly adopted the horse and buffalo hunt as their way of life. They became allies of the Assiniboine in their battle with the Blackfoot to secure control of the Canadian prairies.

The Cree were a particularly superstitious people. Sometimes reduced by periodic shortages of game to occasional acts of cannabalism which, like other Algonkians, they viewed with horror, the Cree lived in great fear of legendary *windigos*, or *wendigos*—human beings transformed into supernatural, man-eating giants after consuming human flesh.

OJIBWA

Mackenzie makes only one brief allusion to the Ojibwa, or Ojibway, in the *Voyages*, but then he had little or no opportunity to meet natives who lived mainly to the north or to the east of Lakes Huron and Superior.

These Indians, whose name was garbled into Chippewa or Chippeway by fur traders, belonged to the huge linguistic group of Algonkian-speaking Indians and were basically a hunting and fishing people. With the possible exception of the Cree, the Ojibwa, "the people whose moccasins have puckered seams," were the largest Indian nation in the continental north. (Even today they number about twenty thousand persons.) They were so numerous and occupied so much territory that they are often identified as forming four main groups or tribes: the Lake Superior Ojibwa, or Salteaux, so called from their habit of foregathering at the falls (sault) of Sault Ste Marie; the Mississauga of Manitoulin Island; the Ottawa of the Georgian Bay region; and the Potawatomi, who lived west of Lake Huron in what is now the state of Michigan.

The Lake Superior Ojibwa were excellent canoe builders and, as trappers and middlemen, had been of great help to the French as the fur trade moved out over the prairies and then into the northern forest.

SIOUX

The Sioux first came to the attention of Europeans in the Jesuit *Relation* of 1640, which reported that they lived in the general vicinity of Sault Ste Marie. But by the late seventeenth century the Ojibwa, using firearms bought from the French, had driven them south and west of the Great Lakes. The Sioux nation never again resided in what is now Canada, although a number of bands chose to cross the 49th parallel and settle permanently in western Canada after retaliation by the United States government for the Sioux victory over Lieutenant-Colonel George Custer and his cavalry regiment at the battle of the Little Big Horn (River) in 1876. Mackenzie mentions the Sioux only occasionally, referring to them at one point as the "Nadowasis," a variant or misspelling of the Ojibwa word "Nadouessioux," which literally means "rattlesnakes" and thus enemies. (The term Sioux is a French Canadian abbreviation of Nadouessioux.)

The Dakota, as the Sioux called themselves, were a large group of Siouan-speaking Indians who finally settled west of the Mississippi, principally along the headwaters of the Missouri. They were a plains people, dependent for almost all their needs on the buffalo. Usually tall, slender, and sinewy, with high cheekbones and beaked noses, they are the legendary Indians of the Wild West and the prototype of the Indian to be seen on the United States five-cent piece. They were a proud, independent people, and it is the powerful Teton division of the Sioux nation that has been immortalized in Western novels and movies.

In Mackenzie's time, the Sioux generally confined their animosities to fighting neighbouring tribes, but in the early and mid-eighteenth century they opposed the French and their Algonkian-speaking allies and often sent raiding parties to disrupt the trade by burning fur posts and ambushing canoe parties. Even in the late eighteenth century, the Sioux made occasional forays into the upper Great Lakes region to kill groups of voyageurs and pillage their canoes.

Bibliographical Notes

1. In item R.G.I. E15A, Public Accounts of the Province of Quebec, 1785, Pt. II.
2. Kennicott, Robert, *Transactions of the Chicago Academy of Sciences*, 1869.
3. Ross, Alexander, *The Fur Hunters of the Far West*, London, 1855.
4. Public Archives of Canada, M.G. II, Series Q, 36-1, pp. 280-310.
5. Public Archives of Canada, M.G. II, Series Q, Vol, 49, p. 357.
6. Landmann, George Thomas, *Adventures and Recollections*, London, 1852.
7. *Ibid.*
8. *Ibid.*
9. From an appendix to the report that accompanied Simcoe's dispatch No. 36 of 11 September 1794, Public Record Office, London.
10. Alexander Henry to John Askin, 18 January 1800, *Collections of the State Historical Society of Wisconsin*, Volume XIX, Madison.
11. John Strachan to Dr. James Brown, 23 October 1802, Public Archives of Ontario.
12. Patrick C. T. White, ed., *Lord Selkirk's Diary, 1803-1804*, Toronto, The Champlain Society, 1958.
13. Public Archives of Canada, M.G. II, Series Q, Vol. 24-2, p. 409.
14. London, Public Record Office, C.O. 42, 47, pp. 649-51.
15. Public Archives of Canada, M.G. II, Series Q, Vol. 50-1, pp. 1-2.
16. William McGillivray to Aeneas Cameron, September 1799, Cameron Papers, courtesy of Mrs. W. F. Mitchell, Toronto.
17. William McGillivray to Aeneas Cameron, 8 May, 1800, Cameron Papers, courtesy of Mrs. W. F. Mitchell, Toronto.
18. F. 3/2, fo. 103, Hudson's Bay Company Archives, London.

19. John Fraser to Simon McTavish, 18 January 1800, Hudson's Bay Company Archives, London.
20. Selkirk, Thomas Douglas, 5th Earl of, *Sketch of the British Fur-Trade in North America, with Observations Relative to the North West Company of Montreal*, London, 1816.
21. De Voto, Bernard, *The Course of Empire*, Boston, Houghton Mifflin, 1952.
22. Isaac Todd to Colonel Green, 15 October, 1804, Public Archives of Canada, Ottawa.
23. De Voto, Bernard, *The Course of Empire*, Boston, Houghton Mifflin, 1952.

Bibliography

The primary source for Mackenzie's writings is W. Kaye Lamb's edition of *The Journals and Letters of Sir Alexander Mackenzie*, published in 1971 for the Hakluyt Society by the Cambridge University Press. (The book also includes "A General History of the Fur Trade from Canada to the North-West".) The original manuscripts of the "General History" and of the journal of the expedition to the Pacific have long since disappeared, and so Dr. Lamb's book reproduces the texts of these as they appeared in the 1801 quarto edition of the *Voyages*. However, a copy of Mackenzie's manuscript of the journal of the first voyage survives today in the British Museum. It is this version of the expedition to the Arctic that appears in Dr. Lamb's book. Also included is every known letter or part of a letter written by Mackenzie. Unfortunately these vary considerably in importance and interest because most of Mackenzie's personal papers were lost when Avoch House was destroyed by fire thirteen years after his death.

Dr. Lamb's Introduction contains an excellent account and analysis of Mackenzie's life, and the Bibliography lists, among other things, sixteen editions of the *Voyages*, including a version on microfilm available from University Microfilms, Ann Arbor, Michigan.

The reader is also advised to consult two other books, each of which reproduces a substantial part of the *Voyages*:

McDonald, T. H., ed., *Exploring the Northwest Territory: Sir Alexander Mackenzie's Journal of a Voyage by Bark Canoe from Lake Athabasca to the Pacific* [sic] *Ocean in the Summer of 1789*, University of Oklahoma Press, 1966.

Sheppe, Walter, ed., *First Man West: Alexander Mackenzie's Journal of his Voyage to the Pacific Coast of Canada in 1793*, McGill University Press, 1962.

Much information on Mackenzie can be gleaned from Sheppe's prologue, epilogue, and appendices. In addition, since Sheppe visited many parts of the route Mackenzie followed, and McDonald travelled by canoe from Fort Chipewyan to the mouth of the Mackenzie River, each editor offers many helpful explanations and observations.

Listed below are biographies of Mackenzie and two associates—Pond and McGillivray—and books on the fur trade, exploration of the continent, and the North American Indian. The literature on each of the latter three is considerable, and I have selected only those titles that are either important or popular enough to be of help and interest to the reader. An asterisk indicates a paperback edition.

Brebner, John Bartlet, *The Explorers of North America, 1492-1806*, *New York, Doubleday, 1955.

Bredin, Thomas, *From Sea to Sea: Alexander Mackenzie*, Toronto, Longmans Canada Limited, 1970.

Campbell, Marjorie W., *The Nor'Westers: the fight for the fur trade* (Great Stories of Canada, No. 4), Toronto, Macmillan, 1954.

Campbell, Marjorie W., *The North West Company*, *Toronto, Macmillan, 1973.

Daniells, Roy, *Alexander Mackenzie and the North West*, *Toronto, Oxford University Press, 1971. London, Faber and Faber, 1969.

Davidson, Gordon Charles, *The North West Company*, University of California Press, 1918.

De Voto, Bernard, *The Course of Empire*, Boston, Houghton Mifflin, 1952.

Bibliography

Gates, Charles M. (ed.), *Five Fur Traders of the Northwest. Being the Narrative of Peter Pond and the diaries of John Macdonnell, Archibald N. McLeod, Hugh Faries, and Thomas Connor*, New edition. St. Paul, Minnesota Historical Society, 1965.

Henry, Alexander [the elder], *Travels and Adventures In Canada and the Indian Territories Between the Years 1760 and 1776*, Edmonton, M. G. Hurtig Ltd., 1969.

Innis, Harold, *The Fur Trade in Canada,** rev. ed., University of Toronto Press, 1956.

Innis, Harold, *Peter Pond: Fur Trader and Adventurer*, Toronto, Irwin and Gordon, 1930.

Jenness, Diamond, *The Indians of Canada*, 7th ed., Ottawa, Queen's Printer, 1967.

Josephy, Alvin M., Jr., *The Indian Heritage of America,** New York, Bantam Books, 1969.

Lamb, W. Kaye, ed., *Sixteen Years in the Indian Country: The Journal of Daniel Williams Harmon, 1800-1816*, Toronto, Macmillan, 1957.

Lambert, Richard, *Trailmaker: The story of Alexander Mackenzie*, Toronto, McClelland & Stewart, 1957.

MacKay, Douglas, *The Honourable Company: a history of the Hudson's Bay Company*, rev. ed., Toronto, McClelland & Stewart, 1949.

Mackenzie, Alexander, *Voyages from Montreal, on the River St. Laurence, through the Continent of North America, to the Frozen and Pacific Oceans; in the Years 1789 and 1793. With a Preliminary Account of the Rise, Progress, and Present State of the Fur Trade of that Country*, various editions.

Masson, L. R., *Les Bourgeois de la Compagnie du Nord-Ouest*, 2 vols., Quebec, 1889-90 [which includes—in English—information on Roderic McKenzie and also some correspondence of Alexander Mackenzie].

Mirsky, Jeannette, *The Westward Crossings: Balboa, Mackenzie, Lewis and Clark,** Chicago, University of Chicago Press, 1970.

Morse, Eric W., *Fur Trade Canoe Routes of Canada/Then and Now*, Ottawa, Queen's Printer, 1969.

Nute, Grace L., *The Voyageur*, reprint edition, St. Paul, Minnesota Historical Society, 1955.

Rich, E. E., *The Fur Trade and The Northwest to 1857*, Toronto, McClelland & Stewart, 1967.

Rich, E. E., *The History of the Hudson's Bay Company, 1670-1870*, 2 vols., London, Hudson's Bay Record Society, 1958-9.

Rich E. E., *Montreal and the Fur Trade*, McGill University Press, 1966.

Saum, Lewis O., *The Fur Trader and the Indian,** Seattle, University of Washington Press, 1965.

Syme, Ronald, *Alexander Mackenzie: Canadian Explorer* (Morrow Junior Books), New York, William Morrow, 1964.

Thomson, Don W., *Men and Meridians: The History of Surveying and Mapping in Canada, Volume 1, Prior to 1867*, Ottawa, Queen's Printer, 1966.

Vail, Philip [pseud.], *The Magnificent Adventures of Alexander Mackenzie*, New York, Dodd, Mead, 1964.

Wade, Mark Sweetan, *Mackenzie of Canada: The Life and Adventures of Alexander Mackenzie, Discoverer*, Edinburgh, William Blackwood, 1927.

Wagner, Henry R., *Peter Pond: Fur Trader and Explorer*, Yale University Library, 1955.

Wallace, W. Stewart, ed., *Documents Relating to the North West Company*, Toronto, The Champlain Society, 1934.

Wallace, W. Stewart, *The Pedlars from Quebec, and Other Papers on the Nor'Westers*, Toronto, The Ryerson Press, 1954.

Warkentin, John, *The Western Interior of Canada: A Record of Geographical Discovery 1612-1917,** Toronto, McClelland & Stewart, 1964.

Woollacott, Arthur P., *Mackenzie and his Voyageurs, by Canoe to the Arctic and the Pacific 1789-93*, London and Toronto, J. M. Dent, 1927.

Wrong, Hume, *Sir Alexander Mackenzie, Explorer and Fur-Trader*, Toronto, Macmillan, 1927.

Wymer, Norman, *With Mackenzie in Canada*, (Adventures in Geography Series), London, Frederick Muller, 1963.

INDEX